INTELLECTUAL FREEDOM MANUAL

Compiled by the
> OFFICE FOR INTELLECTUAL FREEDOM
> *of the*
> AMERICAN LIBRARY ASSOCIATION

53648

AMERICAN LIBRARY ASSOCIATION

Chicago

Library of Congress Cataloging in Publication Data

American Library Association. Office for Intellectural
    Freedom.
    Intellectual freedom manual.

    Bibliography: p.
    1. Libraries--Censorship. I. Title.
Z711.4.A57 1974   323.44   73-22338
ISBN 0-8389-3181-2

Printed in the United States of America
First paperbound edition, November 1975

Contents

Preface   v

Introduction   vii

ALA and Intellectual Freedom:
A Historical Overview   xi

Part 1.   Library Bill of Rights

Library Bill of Rights   3
Interpretations of the "Library Bill of Rights"   13
    Free Access to Libraries for Minors   14
    Statement on Labeling   22
    Expurgation of Library Materials   24
    Sexism, Racism, and Other -isms in Library
        Materials   27
    Reevaluating Library Collections   30
    How Libraries Can Resist Censorship   32
    Resolution on Challenged Materials   39
    Restricted Access to Library Materials   42
    Intellectual Freedom Statement   46

Part 2.   Freedom to Read

The Freedom to Read   3
School Library Bill of Rights   20
Policy on Confidentiality of Library Records   27
Resolution on Governmental Intimidation   32

Part 3.   Intellectual Freedom

Intellectual Freedom: An All-Embracing Concept   3
    Public Libraries and Intellectual Freedom   4
    School Libraries and Intellectual Freedom   11
    Academic Libraries and Intellectual Freedom   14
    Federal Libraries and Intellectual Freedom   17
    State Library Agencies and Intellectual Freedom   19

Part 4.   Before the Censor Comes:
          Essential Preparations

Before the Censor Comes:
    Essential Preparations 3
    Development of a Materials Selection Program 5
    Procedures for Handling Complaints 11
    Public Relations and the Library 15
    The Censor: His Motives and Tactics 21
    Addendum: Participants in Ad Hoc
        Antipornography Organizations 25

Part 5. Intellectual Freedom and the Law
    Librarians and Their Legislators 3

Part 6. Assistance from ALA
    What ALA Can Do to Help the Library
        Combat Censorship 3

    Selected Readings 1

Preface

This manual is designed to answer the many practical questions that confront librarians in applying the principles of intellectual freedom to library service. It is our hope that every librarian will keep this volume on his desk as a convenient reference work. If, for example, he wants to know what the American Library Association can do to help the librarian resist censorship of library materials, or how to handle complaints or simply write an appropriate letter to legislators, he can find help in this volume. If his problem is complex—for example, the development of a materials selection program—he will find practical guidelines on how to tackle the problem.

The first section of the manual offers a different kind of help. "ALA and Intellectual Freedom" explains not only the meaning of intellectual freedom in library service, but also how today's broad concept of intellectual freedom evolved from opposition to book censorship. In parts 1 and 2, Library Bill of Rights and Freedom to Read, the documents and brief histories of ALA's various policies interpreting and supporting the "Library Bill of Rights" also give concrete examples of the kinds of problems librarians can expect to encounter, problems they should anticipate in formulating policy for their own institutions.

Application of the principles and guidelines of this manual cannot assure that the rights of librarians and library users will never be challenged, nor can it guarantee that unexpected difficulties will not arise. But their application to service in every library is absolutely essential if librarians and library users are to escape the whims of the censor and gain the benefits of freedom of expression under the First Amendment.

JUDITH F. KRUG, *Director*
Office for Intellectual Freedom
American Library Association

JAMES A. HARVEY, *Executive Secretary*
Illinois Library Association

ROGER L. FUNK, *Assistant Director*
Office for Intellectual Freedom
American Library Association

PATRICIA R. HARRIS, *Assistant to the Director*
Office for Intellectual Freedom
American Library Association

Introduction

Censorship reflects society's lack of confidence in itself. It is the hallmark of an authoritarian regime. . . .
—JUSTICE POTTER STEWART

In basic terms, intellectual freedom means the right of any person to believe whatever he wants on any subject, and to express his beliefs or ideas in whatever way he thinks appropriate. The freedom to express one's beliefs or ideas, through any mode of communication, becomes virtually meaningless, however, when accessibility to such expressions is denied to other persons. For this reason, the definition of intellectual freedom has a second, integral part: namely, the right of unrestricted access to all information and ideas regardless of the medium of communication used. Intellectual freedom implies a circle, and that circle is broken if either freedom of expression or access to the ideas expressed is stifled.

Intellectual freedom is freedom of the mind, and as such, it is not only a personal liberty, but also a prerequisite for all freedoms leading to action. Moreover, as manifested in the freedoms of speech and press dictates of the First Amendment, intellectual freedom forms the bulwark of our constitutional republic. It is an essential part of the mechanism of government by the people. The right to vote is alone not sufficient to give citizens effective control of official actions and policies. They must also be able to take part in the formation of public opinion by engaging in vigorous and wide-ranging debate on controversial matters. Censorship can only stifle this debate, thus weakening government by the people. In the words of President James Madison:

> A popular government, without popular information, or the means of acquiring it, is but a prologue to a

farce or a tragedy; or, perhaps both. Knowledge will forever govern ignorance; and a people who mean to be their own governors, must arm themselves with the power which knowledge gives.[1]

It is in relation to intellectual freedom that libraries have a special role. Librarians have taken upon themselves the responsibility to provide, through their institutions, all points of view on all questions and issues of our times, and to make these ideas and opinions available to anyone who needs or wants them, regardless of age, race, religion, national origins, or social or political views. These statements should sound familiar; they are basic principles outlined in the "Library Bill of Rights," which serves as the library profession's interpretation of the First Amendment to the United States Constitution.

The freedom of expression guaranteed by the First Amendment and the corollary to that freedom, the freedom to read, are uniquely fulfilled by the library. Any person, regardless of his station, can have access to the materials and information he needs. Of course, libraries are widely recognized as the repositories of civilization, but in order to guarantee that the freedom to read has substance, libraries must also acquire and provide information quite without prejudice or restriction. It is this latter point which gives the "Library Bill of Rights" and its guidance of professional librarianship special importance.

But intellectual freedom cannot bring itself into existence. Librarians must apply the principles of intellectual freedom to activities undertaken daily—materials selection, reference service, reevaluation and, most importantly, collection building. It is in collection activities and their product, the collection, that intellectual freedom must be reflected.

The role of the library as governed by the "Library Bill of Rights" cannot be filled by any other institution of society. Newspapers provide information, but it is perforce abridged and can reflect the prejudices of an editor or publisher. Schools educate, but according to a program designed to fit the many, and one attends schools on the conditions of administrators and educators. It is in the library, and in the library alone, that one can learn to the limits of his abilities and to the limits of what is known.

1. James Madison, letter to W. T. Barry, Aug. 4, 1822, in *The Complete Madison* (New York: Harper, 1953), p.337.

No one—least of all the librarian—should underestimate the importance of this role. If the significance of this role has been overlooked by many, including librarians, perhaps it is because some librarians have been neither vigorous in the application of these principles nor imaginative in the provision of library services. With the application of the principles of intellectual freedom, with vision and imagination, librarians can measure up to their unique task.

ALA and Intellectual Freedom: A Historical Overview

Judith F. Krug and James A. Harvey

At the outset, two myths can be disspelled, namely, that intellectual freedom in libraries is a tradition, and that intellectual freedom has always been a major, if not the major, part of the foundation of library service in the United States. Both myths, assumed by many librarians, are grounded in the belief that librarians support a static concept of intellectual freedom. Nothing, however, could be farther from the truth.

The attitude of librarians toward intellectual freedom has undergone continual change since the late 1800s when, through the American Library Association (ALA), the profession first began to approach such issues with the semblance of a unified voice. However, ALA has never endorsed a uniform definition of "intellectual freedom." Instead, through the Council, ALA's governing body, the Intellectual Freedom Committee (IFC), and the Office for Intellectual Freedom (OIF), ALA has promoted a variety of principles aimed at fostering a favorable climate for intellectual freedom but without the limits imposed by a rigid definition. In effect, this approach has allowed a broad definition capable of meeting the needs of librarians as they arise.

A thrust against censorship of published materials initiated the general definition of intellectual freedom, but from this main trunk numerous branches have continued to spring. One concerns the library user and his access to all the materials in a library collection. Another pertains to the librarian and the practice of his profession, particularly selecting and making available all published materials to all library users, without fear of reprisals. At stake also is the librarian's per-

This chapter is a revised version of the authors' "Intellectual Freedom and Librarianship," in *Encyclopedia of Library and Information Sciences* (New York: Dekker, forthcoming). Printed by permission. Copyright © Marcel Dekker, Inc.

sonal intellectual freedom, his participation in the democratic process, his right to express himself freely and to pursue his chosen life style without fear of threats to his professional position. Yet another aspect of intellectual freedom encompasses the library as an institution and its role in social change and education. Of particular importance is the question of "advocacy" versus "neutrality." Can a library committed to intellectual freedom and to providing materials that represent all points of view also support one point of view?

Each of these main branches has sprouted a plethora of twigs, and viewed in its entirety the tree makes anything other than an issue oriented approach nearly impossible. Consequently, the profession's stance on intellectual freedom has sometimes lagged behind society at large; most often it has paralleled public opinion; and, occasionally, it has anticipated changes in taste, mores, and social issues and has taken positions in advance of the rest of the citizenry.

CENSORSHIP OF PUBLISHED MATERIALS

The catalyst spurring librarians to take initial steps toward supporting intellectual freedom was the censorship of specific publications. "Censorship," in this context, means not only deletion or excision of parts of published materials, but also efforts to ban, prohibit, suppress, proscribe, remove, label, or restrict materials. Opposition to these activities emanated from the belief that freedom of the mind is basic to the functioning and maintenance of democracy as practiced in the United States. Such democracy assumes that educated, free individuals possess powers of discrimination and are to be trusted to determine their own actions. It assumes further that the best guarantee of effective and continuing self-government is a thoroughly informed electorate capable of making real choices. Denying the opportunity of choice, for fear it may be used unwisely, destroys freedom itself. Opposition to censorship derives naturally from the library's historical role as an educational institution providing materials that develop individuals' abilities, interests, and knowledge. Censorship denies the opportunity to choose from all possible alternatives, and thereby violates intellectual freedom. The library profession has aimed to ensure every individual's freedom of the mind so that society as a whole benefits. Even in this central area, however, the professional position has fluctuated, being influenced by such factors as taste, quality, responsibility, morality, legality, and purpose.

One early incident concerning censorship, and involving a substantial number of librarians, occurred in 1924 when the Librarians' Union of the American Federation of Labor reported that Carnegie libraries fostered "a system under which only books approved in a certain manner may be placed on Carnegie Library shelves and that amounts to censorship and is so intended."[1] The ALA Executive Board considered the union's charges and offered to enlist volunteers to investigate the claims. Apparently, however, the union did not act upon the offer, and the matter was not considered further by the Executive Board.

In 1929, the Association indicated its future approach to censorship when the ALA Executive Board studied a proposed federal tariff bill and opposed prohibition of importing materials "advocating or urging treason, insurrection, or forcible resistance to any law of the U.S. . . . or any obscene book, paper, etc." The board's opposition was based

> on the grounds that this clause creates an effective censorship over foreign literature; will ban many of the classics on modern economics; will keep out material relating to revolutions in foreign countries; will indirectly stop the reprinting of such books by our own publishers; and is a reflection upon the intelligence of the American people by implying that they are so stupid and untrustworthy that they cannot read about revolutions without immediately becoming traitors and revolutionaries themselves; and because the question of social policy is withdrawn from the ordinary courts and placed in the hands of officials primarily chosen for their special qualifications in dealing with the administrative details of tariff laws.[2]

Ironically, just four years later, when the Executive Board received a letter requesting that the Association "take some action in regard to the burning of books in Germany by the Hitler regime," the matter was "considered briefly but it was the sense of the meeting that no action should be taken."[3]

In 1934, the Association recorded its first protest against the banning of a specific publication, *You and Machines*, a pamphlet by William Ogburn. Prepared for use in Civilian Conservation Corps camps under a grant from the American

1. American Library Association, "Minutes of Executive Board Meetings," mimeographed, 3:20 (Sept. 29, 1924).
2. Ibid., 5:11 (Jan. 1, 1930).
3. Ibid., 6:214 (Oct. 15, 1933).

Council on Education, the pamphlet was denied circulation by the camps' director, who believed it would induce a philosophy of despair and a desire to destroy existing economic and political structures. Initially, the ALA president and executive secretary wrote a joint letter to President Roosevelt stating that "[governmental] censorship on a publication of this character written by a man of recognized authority is unthinkable."[4] At its next meeting, the board discussed the banning further and appointed a committee to draft another letter for approval by the ALA Council. The result was a formal request that President Roosevelt "make it possible for the U.S. Commissioner of Education and the Education Director of the Civilian Conservation Corps to direct the educational policies to be operative in these camps and to make available the reading matter essential in a modern program of education."[5]

These examples illustrate the Association's wavering position and reflect the ambivalent attitude of the profession as a whole regarding censorship. A review of library literature reveals relatively few articles on intellectual freedom prior to the 1930s, and many of the articles that did appear supported censorship and only quibbled over the degree and nature of it. Typical was the opinion of ALA President Arthur E. Bostwick, whose inaugural address at the 1908 Annual Conference included these remarks:

> "Some are born great; some achieve greatness; some have greatness thrust upon them." It is in this way that the librarian has become a censor of literature. . . . Books that distinctly commend what is wrong, that teach how to sin and tell how pleasant sin is, sometimes with and sometimes without the added sauce of impropriety, are increasingly popular, tempting the author to imitate them, the publishers to produce, the bookseller to exploit. Thank Heaven they do not tempt the librarian.[6]

Given the multiplicity of professional attitudes toward censorship of print materials, it is not surprising that censorship of nonprint media was once viewed as completely outside the concerns of the profession. For example, as late as 1938, the ALA Executive Board believed it was inappropriate

4. Ibid., 7:89 (Dec. 27, 1934).
5. Ibid., 7:48–49 (Dec. 27, 1934).
6. Arthur E. Bostwick, "The Librarian as Censor," *ALA Bulletin* 2:113 (Sept. 1908).

to protest when the Federal Communications Commission forced a radio station to defend its broadcast of Eugene O'Neill's *Beyond the Horizon*.[7]

The Association's basic position in opposition to censorship finally emerged in the late 1930s when John Steinbeck's *Grapes of Wrath* became the target of censorship pressures around the country. It was banned from libraries in East St. Louis, Illinois; Camden, New Jersey; Bakersfield, California, and other localities. While some objected to the "immorality" of the work, most opposed the social views advanced by the author.

ALA's initial response to the pressures against *The Grapes of Wrath* was the adoption in 1939 of the "Library's Bill of Rights," the precursor of the present "Library Bill of Rights," the profession's basic policy statement on intellectual freedom involving library materials. (See Library Bill of Rights, pt.1, p.3–12.)

In 1940, one year after adoption of the "Library's Bill of Rights," the Association established the Intellectual Freedom Committee. (Originally called the Committee on Intellectual Freedom to Safeguard the Rights of Library Users to Freedom of Inquiry, the Committee's name was shortened by Council action in 1948 to Committee on Intellectual Freedom and inverted through usage to Intellectual Freedom Committee.) The 1940 charge to the IFC was "to recommend such steps as may be necessary to safeguard the rights of library users in accordance with the Bill of Rights and the 'Library's Bill of Rights' as adopted by Council."[8] Although the IFC's role has varied, its main function has been to recommend policies concerning intellectual freedom, especially—but not limited to—matters involving violations of the "Library Bill of Rights." Although its original statement of authority referred only to library users, in reality the IFC became active in promoting intellectual freedom for librarians and patrons as well. Its diversified role was recognized and formalized in 1970 when the Council approved a revised statement of authority:

> To recommend such steps as may be necessary to safeguard the rights of library users, libraries, and librarians, in accordance with the First Amendment to the

7. American Library Association, "Minutes of Executive Board Meetings," mimeographed, 10:48 (Oct. 5, 1938).

8. "Cincinnati Proceedings—Council," *ALA Bulletin* 34:P-37 (Aug. 1940).

United States Constitution and the *Library Bill of Rights* as adopted by the ALA Council. To work closely with the Office for Intellectual Freedom and with other units and officers of the Association in matters touching intellectual freedom and censorship.[9]

The original "Library's Bill of Rights" focused on unbiased book selection, a balanced collection, and open meeting rooms. It did not mention censorship or removal of materials at the behest of groups or individuals. Over the years, however, the document has been revised, amended and interpreted, often in response to specific situations with general implications. The first change, a 1944 amendment against banning materials considered "factually correct," was occasioned by attacks on *Under Cover*, an exposé of Nazi organizations in the United States, and *Strange Fruit*, a novel about interracial love. Reference to "factually correct" was later dropped, but the directive against removal of materials remained. Opposition to censorship of nonprint media was amended to the document in 1951 because of attacks on films alleged to promote communism. To combat suppression of communist materials or other allegedly "subversive" publications, the Association issued its "Statement on Labeling" (pt.1, p.18–22), which states that designating materials "subversive" is subtle censorship because such a label predisposes readers against the materials. Responding to pressures against materials about civil rights activities, a 1967 amendment to the "Library Bill of Rights" warned against excluding materials because of the social views of the authors. In its 1971 "Resolution on Challenged Materials," the Association counsels libraries not to remove challenged materials unless after an adversary hearing in a court of law the materials are judged to be outside the protection of the First Amendment. (See Resolution on Challenged Materials, pt.1, p.39–41.)

The present "Library Bill of Rights," with its interpretive documents, recognizes that censorship of any materials, in any guise, eventually affects the library. The bill therefore provides principles for libraries to support, in the broadest sense, in order to oppose censorship and promote intellectual freedom. Referring directly to censorship practices, the bill states that no library materials should be "excluded because of the race or nationality or the social, political, or religious

9. American Library Association, *Handbook of Organization, 1971–1972* (Chicago: ALA, n.d.), p.13.

xvi

views of the authors," and that "no library materials should be proscribed or removed because of partisan or doctrinal disapproval" (pt.1, p.11).

On its face, the profession's view of intellectual freedom is a pure one, based on a strict reading of the First Amendment to the U.S. Constitution, which states that "Congress shall make no law . . . abridging freedom of speech, or of the press." Within certain limits, for example, laws governing libel and "fighting words," the position relies on the extension of First Amendment rights, through the Fourteenth Amendment, to all library services governed by public agencies. In actual practice, the purist position sometimes gives way to compromises by individual librarians, resulting in removal, labeling, or covert nonselection of certain materials. Changing circumstances necessitate constant review of the "Library Bill of Rights" and often result in position statements to clarify the document's application. (See Interpretations of the "Library Bill of Rights," pt.1, p.13–50.)

If followed by librarians and governing bodies, however, the Association's policy statements provide an effective means of helping to prevent library censorship. Ideally, application of these policies to materials selection, circulation practices, and complaint handling establishes the library as an indispensable information source for individuals exercising their freedom of inquiry.

FREE ACCESS TO LIBRARY MATERIALS

Access to library collections and services is another concern of the profession. For intellectual freedom to flourish, opposition to censorship of materials is not enough. Free access to materials for every member of the community must also be assured. ALA first recognized this in the 1939 "Library's Bill of Rights," which included a proviso that library meeting rooms be available on equal terms to all groups in the community regardless of the beliefs and affiliations of their members. In 1967, this doctrine was amended by the qualification, "provided that the meetings be open to the public."[10]

Another policy on free access emerged from a study of segregation made by the Association's Special Committee on

10. American Library Association, *Policies, Procedures and Position Statements* (2d ed.; Chicago: ALA, 1970), p.63.

Civil Liberties during the late 1950s. One result of the study was a 1961 amendment to the "Library Bill of Rights," stating that "the rights of an individual to the use of a library should not be denied or abridged because of his race, religion, national origins or political views." This amendment was broadened in 1967, when "social views" and "age" were incorporated to emphasize other areas of potential discrimination.[11] "Social views" was added to safeguard access for advocates of causes viewed unfavorably by segments of the community. "Age" was included to resolve a long-standing debate on the right of minors to have access to libraries on the same basis as adults. It should be noted that the addition of "age" illustrates one instance in which the library profession acted well in advance of public opinion.

In 1971, at the urging of the Task Force on Gay Liberation of the Social Responsibilities Round Table, the Association supported the intellectual freedom of other groups of library users. ALA recommended that libraries and ALA members strenuously combat discrimination in serving any individual from a minority, whether it be an ethnic, sexual, religious, or of any other kind of minority.

Another aspect of the library patron's access to materials was broached in 1970 when the Internal Revenue Service requested permission from several libraries to examine circulation records to determine the names of persons reading materials about explosives and guerilla warfare. The Association responded through its "Policy on the Confidentiality of Library Records," urging libraries to designate such records as confidential and accessible only "pursuant to such process, order, or subpoena as may be authorized under the authority of, and pursuant to, federal, state, or local law relating to civil, criminal, or administrative discovery procedures or legislative investigatory power" (pt.2, p.31). The rationale of the policy was that circulation records are purely circumstantial evidence that a patron has read a book, and that fear of persecution or prosecution may restrain users from borrowing any conceivably controversial materials, for whatever purpose.

The question of library records and the confidentiality of relationships between librarians and library users arose again in 1971 regarding the "use of grand jury procedure to intimidate anti-Vietnam War activists and people seeking justice for minority communities." In response, the Association

11. Ibid.

asserted "the confidentiality of the professional relationships of librarians to the people they serve, that these relationships be respected in the same manner as medical doctors to their patients, lawyers to their clients, priests to the people they serve," and that "no librarian would lend himself to a role as informant, whether of voluntarily revealing circulation records or identifying patrons and their reading habits" (pt.2, p.33).

Through the Association's various position statements, the profession has established a code of free access to services and materials for all library users. Opposed to using the library as a means of intimidating patrons, the profession has, in effect, enhanced the intellectual freedom of the library user by providing not only all materials requested, but also free and equal access to all materials without fear of recrimination for pursuing one's interests.

THE LIBRARIAN AND INTELLECTUAL FREEDOM

While the profession, through ALA, formulates policies to help ensure a climate favorable to intellectual freedom, the individual librarian is the key to achieving the end result. His adherence to the "Library Bill of Rights" is the only means of effecting the profession's goals. Consequently, the concept of intellectual freedom also considers the individual librarian's intellectual freedom, both in pursuit of his professional responsibilities and in his personal life. Several agencies within or closely affiliated with ALA, accordingly, encourage and protect the librarians' commitment to the principles of intellectual freedom.

From 1940 until 1967, most of such activities were centered in the Intellectual Freedom Committee. For many years it not only recommended policies but also directed a variety of educational efforts including collecting and publicizing information about censorship incidents, sponsoring censorship exhibits at conferences, conducting preconferences on intellectual freedom themes, and planning complementary programs to further the Association's goals regarding intellectual freedom.

One of these complementary programs is the Office for Intellectual Freedom, established in December 1967. OIF evolved finally from a 1965 preconference on intellectual freedom held in Washington, D.C. That meeting recommended establishing an ALA headquarters unit to conduct and coordinate the Association's intellectual freedom activities and to provide continuity for the total program. The goal of OIF is to educate librarians on the importance of intellectual freedom, relieving the IFC of this task and allowing it to concentrate on developing policy. The Office serves as the administrative arm of the Committee and bears the responsibility for implementing ALA policies on intellectual freedom, as approved by the Council. The philosophy of the Office is based on the premise that if librarians are to appreciate the importance of intellectual freedom they must first understand the concept as it relates to the individual, the institution, and, indeed, the functioning of society. Believing that with understanding comes the ability to teach others, the Office maintains a broad program of informational publications, projects, and services.

The regular OIF publications are the bimonthly *Newsletter on Intellectual Freedom* and the monthly *OIF Memorandum*. In addition, the Office prepares special materials from time to time and distributes documents, articles, and all ALA policy statements concerning intellectual freedom. As part of its informational program, OIF also maintains and distributes the OIF exhibits, collections of materials representing virtually the entire spectrum of social and political thought. These exhibits are available for display at national, state, and local conferences, workshops, seminars, and other meetings involving intellectual freedom.

The Office advises and consults with librarians confronting potential or actual censorship problems. Telephone and letter requests about materials which have drawn the censorial attention of an individual or group in the community prompt efforts to give appropriate assistance. The Office also coordinates the Intellectual Freedom Committee's relations with other agencies having similar concerns. These include the Intellectual Freedom Subcommittee of the American Library Trustee Association, the Ad Hoc Committee on Intellectual Freedom of the American Association of School Librarians, and state library association intellectual freedom committees. Close contact with nonlibrary organizations, such as the Association of American Publishers, the American Civil Liberties Union, the National Education Association, and others, is also maintained.

The Intellectual Freedom Committee and the Office for Intellectual Freedom are the two primary agencies for establishing and promoting the Association's positions on questions involving intellectual freedom. However, soon after adoption of the "Library Bill of Rights" and establishment of the Intellectual Freedom Committee, the profession realized that more than just informational sources were needed to foster the practice of intellectual freedom in libraries. Some members called for a "policing" effort to publicize censorship problems and bring pressure upon authorities to correct conditions conducive to censorship. As early as the 1948 ALA Annual Conference in Atlantic City, Dr. Robert D. Leigh, director of the Public Library Inquiry, addressed the Council and recommended that "some responsible group" be created to investigate reports of library censorship, to make public reports of investigations, to give possible aid to professionals who become victims of censorship, and in extreme cases, to exercise "a professional boycott against the libraries of censoring authorities."[12] Some of Dr. Leigh's recommendations were debated for nearly twenty years before a national resolution of the problems began to emerge. As a first substantive step, in 1969 the Association adopted its "Program of Action in Support of the Library Bill of Rights."

The first "Program of Action," developed by the IFC and approved by the Council, created a mechanism whereby complaints about censorship incidents were reported to the Office for Intellectual Freedom and acted upon by the Committee. Such complaints were studied by the Office and the Committee to determine whether or not they involved intellectual freedom problems within the scope of the "Library Bill of Rights." If the complaint fell under the "Program of Action," the Office and the Committee attempted to mediate, arbitrate, or provide appropriate assistance to effect a just resolution of the problem. If these means failed, one prerogative of the Committee chairman was to establish a fact-finding team to investigate further. After such a fact-finding, the team reported its findings to the IFC for review. Further substantive action required a recommendation by the Committee to the ALA Executive Board. Under a "Sanctions Policy" adopted in 1971, the IFC could recommend publication of a summary of the report, it could recommend publication of the entire report, or it could recommend various other sanctions against groups or individuals violating the spirit of the "Library Bill of Rights." The ALA Executive Board made the final disposition of the Committee's recommendations. (See pt.6, p.6–7 for details of the procedure.)

12. Robert D. Leigh, "Intellectual Freedom," *ALA Bulletin* 42:369 (Sept. 1948).

From 1969 to 1971, in response to requests for action, three fact-findings were undertaken by the IFC. The first major case was brought by Joan Bodger. An extensive investigation explored Mrs. Bodger's charge that she had been fired from the Missouri State Library because of her public support of intellectual freedom. She had written a letter to a local newspaper protesting the suppression of an underground newspaper. The Committee concluded that her allegations were correct and recommended publication of the complete report in *American Libraries*. The Executive Board approved, and the report of the Bodger fact-finding team appeared in the July/August 1970 issue of *American Libraries*, vindicating Mrs. Bodger and deploring the Missouri State Library Commission's actions which resulted in her firing.

The other two requests for action also entailed fact-finding studies, after which the Committee found it could not support charges contained in the complaints. Reports summarizing the two cases were published in *American Libraries*.[13]

The three complaints investigated under the "Program of Action" made it clear that cases involving intellectual freedom might also raise issues of tenure, academic status, ethical practices, and a variety of other matters. The difficulty of focusing only on intellectual freedom increased in late 1970 when a complaint was received from J. Michael McConnell, who was denied a position at the University of Minnesota Library shortly after his well-publicized application for a marriage license to marry another male. Charging that the university discriminated against him because of his homosexuality, Mr. McConnell appealed to the IFC, claiming his case fell under the "Program of Action." To support his claim, he cited the 1946 ALA "Statement of Principles of Intellectual Freedom and Tenure for Librarians," which states: "Intellectual freedom precludes partisan political control of appointments and makes it possible for librarians to devote themselves to the practice of their profession without fear of interference or of dismissal for political, religious, racial, marital, or other unjust reasons."

The IFC did not dispute Mr. McConnell's claim that his case fell under the scope of the 1946 policy statement. It disagreed, however, that it came within the jurisdiction of the "Program of Action," because that mechanism dealt only with violations of the "Library Bill of Rights." The Commit-

13. Rosichan summary, *American Libraries* 1:433 (May 1970) and Scott summary, *American Libraries* 2:316–17 (March 1971).

tee attempted to resolve the problem by rewriting the "Program of Action" to allow jurisdiction over all ALA policies on intellectual freedom. The revision, completed during a special December 1970 meeting of the IFC, was to come before the Council for approval in January 1971. But at its Midwinter Meeting, the Committee again revised the document to include all ALA policies on intellectual freedom and tenure. It was then pointed out that both the Library Administration Division (LAD), and the Association of College and Research Libraries (ACRL) claimed vested interests in investigations, particularly those involving tenure of academic librarians. The complex jurisdictional problems resulted in an appeal to ALA President Lillian Bradshaw to take steps immediately to develop a central investigatory agency for the entire Association. Moving swiftly, Mrs. Bradshaw appointed a membership group representing various interests. In June 1971, the group presented the "Program of Action for Mediation, Arbitration, and Inquiry" to the Council, which adopted it and rescinded the first "Program of Action."

The new "Program of Action" established a Staff Committee on Mediation, Arbitration, and Inquiry (SCMAI), made up of staff representatives of the Office for Intellectual Freedom, LAD, ACRL, one member-at-large, and the ALA executive director, who serves as chairman. Under the new "Program of Action," the SCMAI functions somewhat as the IFC did under the old document. In addition to intellectual freedom problems, however, the new committee handles cases involving tenure, professional status, fair employment practices, ethical practices, and due process as set forth in ALA policies.

Through their respective responsibilities and cooperative efforts the Intellectual Freedom Committee, the Office for Intellectual Freedom, and the Staff Committee on Mediation, Arbitration, and Inquiry comprise three-quarters of the Association's program in support and defense of intellectual freedom. The other part is made up of the Freedom to Read Foundation, created outside the structure of ALA but closely affiliated through the Foundation's board of trustees and executive director, who also serves as the director of the Office for Intellectual Freedom. The incorporation of the Foundation in November 1969 was ALA's response to librarians who increasingly wanted defense machinery to protect their jobs from jeopardy when they undertook to challenge violations of intellectual freedom. Another primary objective in establishing the Foundation was to have a means through which librarians and other concerned individuals and groups could begin to set legal precedents for the freedom to read.

A program of education on the importance of, and the necessity for a commitment to, the principles of intellectual freedom requires assurance that such a commitment will not result in reprisals, such as legal prosecution, financial loss, or personal damage. The Freedom to Read Foundation attempts to provide that assurance through financial and legal assistance and judicial challenge of restrictive legislation, thereby helping to create a favorable climate for intellectual freedom. Through the provision of financial and legal assistance, the Foundation attempts to negate the necessity for librarians to make the difficult choice between practical expediency (that is, maintaining a job) and upholding principles, such as in selecting materials for library collections. Through its various projects and grants, the Foundation hopes to establish those principles enunciated in the "Library Bill of Rights" as legal precedents, rather than as mere paper policies.

Affiliated with the Freedom to Read Foundation is the LeRoy C. Merritt Humanitarian Fund, created in 1970. The Merritt Fund was established by the Foundation's board of trustees in recognition of the individual's need for subsistence and other support when his position is jeopardized or lost as a result of defending intellectual freedom. This special fund offers immediate assistance even prior to the development of all pertinent facts in a particular case.

The philosophy underlying the Freedom to Read Foundation and the Merritt Fund is perhaps best expressed in the "Intellectual Freedom Statement" (adopted June 1971 by the ALA Council), which states in part:

> Both as citizens and professionals, we will strive by all legitimate means open to us to be relieved of the threat of personal, economic, and legal reprisals resulting from our support and defense of the principles of intellectual freedom.
>
> Those who refuse to compromise their ideals in support of intellectual freedom have often suffered dismissals from employment, forced resignations, boycotts of products and establishments, and other invidious forms of punishment. We perceive the admirable, often lonely, refusal to succumb to threats of punitive action as the highest form of true professionalism: dedication to the cause of intellectual freedom and the preservation of vital human and civil liberties. [See pt.1, p.50.]

In the combined forces of the Intellectual Freedom Committee, the Office for Intellectual Freedom, the Staff Committee on Mediation, Arbitration, and Inquiry, and the Freedom to Read Foundation, along with the LeRoy C. Merritt Humanitarian Fund, the library profession has available a complete program to support the practice of intellectual freedom. However, the profession has not yet achieved the same success in a closely related area, the area of the librarian's personal rather than professional intellectual freedom. The question of what support should be given to librarians who suffer professionally because of personal beliefs and actions has been approached in individual cases but has not been resolved by any means.

One of the first instances involving potential recriminations in a professional capacity due to personal beliefs occurred in the late 1940s, with the advent of "loyalty oaths" and "loyalty programs" designed to ferret out Communists and "subversives." The Intellectual Freedom Committee faced the loyalty issue with its "Policy on Loyalty Programs," first adopted by the Council in 1948 and revised in 1951. When another case arose in Florida in 1969, the "Policy on Loyalty Programs" was reexamined and again revised. The last revision, adopted by the Council in January 1971, states, in part, that: "The American Library Association strongly protests loyalty programs which inquire into a library employee's thoughts, reading matter, associates, or membership in organizations, unless a particular person's definite actions warrant such investigation. We condemn loyalty oaths as a condition of employment and investigations which permit the discharge of an individual without a fair hearing."[14]

In 1969, another incident arose involving a librarian who lost his position because of actions, based on personal beliefs, taken in his capacity as a private citizen. T. Ellis Hodgin was fired as city librarian of Martinsville, Virginia, shortly after he joined a lawsuit challenging the constitutionality of a religious education course taught in the city school his daughter attended. He had also been active in civil rights efforts. Mr. Hodgin's situation sparked a controversy among librarians, resulting in a recommendation from the Intellectual Freedom Subcommittee of the Activities Committee on New Directions for ALA (ACONDA) that:

14. "Resolution on Loyalty Investigations," *American Libraries* 2:270 (March 1971).

The scope of intellectual freedom encompasses considerably more than just the freedom to read. Support must also be rendered to the librarian who is fired for sporting a beard, for engaging in civil rights activities, etc., etc. And he should not have to claim "poverty" in order to receive it.[15]

The recommendation, however, was not approved as part of the final ACONDA report.

Some concerned librarians responded to Mr. Hodgin's plight by organizing the National Freedom Fund for Librarians (NFFL) which collected several thousand dollars to aid him. (When the NFFL disbanded in 1971, its cash balance was sent to the LeRoy C. Merritt Humanitarian Fund.)

Mr. Hodgin also appealed to the Freedom to Read Foundation for assistance to defray the financial hardship he suffered due to the loss of his position. In June 1970, the Foundation's executive committee awarded his $500 "for having suffered in his defense of freedom of speech as a result of which he lost his position as a librarian. Inasmuch as it is the obligation of the librarian to protect free speech and a free press through his work as a librarian, it is then particularly appropriate that, when he is deprived of his job because of his own exercise of free speech, the Freedom to Read Foundation assist him in his defense of his freedom."[16] A second grant of $500 was made to Mr. Hodgin in January 1971, for the specific purpose of perfecting an appeal of his suit for reinstatement to the U.S. Supreme Court.

The limits of intellectual freedom were again debated by the profession when the previously mentioned case of J. Michael McConnell arose in 1970. The Intellectual Freedom Committee found that Mr. McConnell's rights "under the First Amendment have been violated" because he met reprisals for freely expressing his sexual preference.[17] On that basis, the LeRoy C. Merritt Humanitarian Fund granted $500 to help defray financial hardship occasioned by his inability to find another job.

15. American Library Association, Activities Committee on New Directions for ALA, "Final Report and Subcommittee Reports, June 1970," mimeographed, p.53.

16. "Hodgin Appeal Rests with U.S. Supreme Court," *Freedom to Read Foundation News* 1:5 (Fall 1971).

17. David K. Berninghausen, "Report of the Intellectual Freedom Committee to Council, Dallas, June 25, 1971," *American Libraries* 2:891 (Sept. 1971).

While Mr. Hodgin, Mr. McConnell, and others in similar positions received some support from the profession, the question of how far librarians in general are willing to extend the scope of intellectual freedom for the benefit of their colleagues is far from settled. At times, the question may seem only semantic or procedural, but in either case—as with the whole concept of intellectual freedom—the problem is approachable only on a case-by-case and issue-by-issue basis.

THE LIBRARY AND INTELLECTUAL FREEDOM

Each aspect of intellectual freedom in libraries which has been discussed to this point has involved people—the library user and his access to all published materials and the librarian and his practice of his professional and/or personal intellectual freedom. One last branch of intellectual freedom remains to be examined, that being the library as an institution and the nature of its role in social change and education. Continually debated within the profession and the American Library Association, the issue has been summarized as "neutrality versus advocacy." In essence, the question is, Can libraries, as institutions, advocate social or political causes and still maintain their image as providers of views representing all sides of all questions?

Whenever the question is raised, it initiates further queries. For example, What constitutes advocating a cause—biased book selection, biased displays, prejudicial assignment of library meeting rooms? Or, What constitutes a cause—peace, ecology, democracy? If a library sponsors a display of books on peace, in order to maintain neutrality must it also sponsor a display on war? The questions are complex, and the answers have shown no uniformity whatsoever. The American Library Association itself has vacillated on the main issue, reaching only a partial resolution in the late 1960s and the early 1970s.

At the 1969 Annual Conference in Atlantic City, the membership and the Council debated whether or not the Association should take a public stand opposing the war in Vietnam or opposing deployment of an antiballistic missile system (ABM). It was argued that political and moral issues are so deeply entangled with education and library issues, that institutions such as ALA and libraries are obligated to take such positions. Those who opposed such positions argued in favor of neutrality on questions not directly related to libraries.

They argued that intellectual freedom for those librarians opposed to the majority view would be violated if the Association attempted to take stands on social and political issues. They further maintained that they had tradition on their side since the Association had always declined to take a stand on issues not directly related to libraries. That argument, of course, was incorrect. The Association had previously taken stands in some instances and refused in others.

In June 1921, for example, the ALA Council espoused a very decided position on the question of disarmament after the First World War. In a strong resolution, the Council stated:

> WHEREAS, The members of the American Library Association had full demonstration of the pain and pinch that belongs to war and the increased cost of all necessities, both personal and professional, caused thereby; and
>
> WHEREAS, The exigencies of international conditions brought about by the cost of war is appalling from every standpoint; and
>
> WHEREAS, We believe the examples of the United States in this matter will be followed by other nations—therefore be it
>
> RESOLVED, That the American Library Association urges upon the president of the United States and Congress the initiative of a movement leading to a reduction of armament at the earliest possible moment; and be it further
>
> RESOLVED, That a request be made by the members of the American Library Association to their individual congressman for such action and that a record be made of the replies.[18]

However, in 1928, when faced by a request from the American Civil Liberties Union that ALA adopt "one or more resolutions on civil liberty, the ALA Executive Board declined, saying the Association "does not take actions on questions outside the library and bibliographic field."[19] That was similar to the philosophy which prevailed in 1969, when the Vietnam and ABM resolutions failed to pass the Council. The question arose again, though, at the 1970 and 1971 Midwinter Meetings and Annual Conferences. After a great deal of de-

18. *ALA Bulletin* 15:169 (July 1921).
19. American Library Association, *Minutes of Executive Board Meetings* 6:142 (May 29, 1928).

bate, the Council voted at its 1970 Annual Conference in Detroit to "define the broad social responsibilities of ALA in terms of . . . the willingness of ALA to take a position on current critical issues with the relationship to libraries and library service clearly set forth in the position statements."[20]

In line with this policy, a carefully reworded resolution opposing the war in Vietnam was adopted by the Council one year later:

> WHEREAS, The stated objective of the American Library Association is the promotion and improvement of library service and librarianship; and
>
> WHEREAS, Continued and improved library service to the American public requires sustained support from the public monies; and
>
> WHEREAS, The continuing U.S. involvement in the conflict in Southeast Asia has so distorted our national priorities as to reduce substantially the funds appropriated for educational purposes, including support for library services to the American people; and
>
> WHEREAS, Continued commitment of U.S. arms, troops, and other military support has not contributed to the solution of this conflict, be it therefore
>
> RESOLVED, That the American Library Association call upon the president of the United States to take immediately those steps necessary to terminate all U.S. military involvement in the present conflict in Southeast Asia by December 31, 1971, and to insure the reallocation of national resources to meet pressing domestic needs.[21]

With approval of the Vietnam resolution, the Association seemed to give broader interpretation to the old "library and bibliographic field." However, this more permissive interpretation still did not resolve the more basic question of whether libraries themselves should follow the course of neutrality or advocacy.

MEASURING THE PROFESSION'S RESPONSE

The foregoing discussion illustrates that anything other than an issue oriented definition of intellectual freedom is

20. *American Libraries* 1:674 (July–Aug. 1970).
21. "Resolution on Southeast Asia Conflict," *American Libraries* 2:826 (Sept. 1971).

impossible. At the present time the profession uniformly disdains censorship of published materials, print or nonprint. The attitude toward user access is somewhat uniform, but contains a great deal of dissent on the question of access for minors to all the materials in a library collection. On the question of the librarian's professional practice of intellectual freedom, there is near agreement that every effort should be made to encourage and protect this aspect of librarianship. The librarian's personal intellectual freedom, on and off the job, presents some points of agreement, but major areas of dissent still exist. The same is true in the area of institutional neutrality vs. advocacy.

One conclusion from a review of the history, status and future of intellectual freedom in libraries is that the American Library Association's positions and programs provide one of the few gauges for measuring the profession's response to the problems of defining, promoting, and defending the concept. ALA's evolving position reflects the steady emergence of a philosophy from the entire library community. While that philosophy exhibits some loose ends, its core grows firmer, based on a history of trial-and-error and forced response to a changing social climate. The philosophy is young, too young to be rooted in tradition, but, gradually, it has gained recognition as the substance of the total philosophy shaping library service in the United States.

Library Bill of Rights

Library Bill of Rights

The "Library Bill of Rights" constitutes the American Library Association's basic policy on intellectual freedom. The bill derives from a statement originally developed by Forrest Spaulding, librarian of the Des Moines Public Library, and adopted by that library on November 21, 1938, as the "Library's Bill of Rights."

Now when indications in many parts of the world point to growing intolerance, suppression of free speech and censorship, affecting the rights of minorities and individuals, the Board of Trustees of the Des Moines Public Library reaffirms these basic policies governing a free public library to serve the best interests of Des Moines and its citizens.

1. Books and other reading matter selected for purchase from public funds shall be chosen from the standpoint of value and interest to the people of Des Moines, and in no case shall selection be based on the race or nationality, political, or religious views of the writers.

2. As far as available material permits, all sides of controversial questions shall be represented equally in the selection of books on subjects about which differences of opinion exist.

3. Official publications and/or propaganda of organized religious, political, fraternal, class, or regional sects, societies, or similar groups, and of institutions controlled by such, are solicited as gifts and will be made available to library users without discrimination. This policy is made necessary because of the meager funds available for the purchase of books and reading matter. It is obviously impossible to purchase the publications of all such groups and it would be unjust discrimination to purchase those of some and not of others.

3

4. Library meeting rooms shall be available on equal terms to all organized nonprofit groups for open meetings to which no admission fee is charged and from which no one is excluded.

The document approved by the ALA Council at the 1939 Annual Conference in San Francisco as the "Library's Bill of Rights" retained the spirit of the Des Moines Public Library policy, but differed from the original in several respects. The principal differences concerned Articles 2, 3, and 4 of the Des Moines policy. In Article 2, reference to equal representation "in the selection of books on subjects about which differences of opinions exist" was changed to "fair and adequate" representation. This change recognized the impossibility of equal representation in terms of numbers of volumes on a particular subject. Article 3 of the Des Moines policy was completely deleted because it dealt with the individual budget, needs, and purposes of a specific library. As such, it was inappropriate for a document to be applied nationwide.

Article 4 of the Des Moines policy, concerning the use of library meeting rooms, was revised extensively before approval by the Council. An introductory phrase establishing the library as "an institution to educate for democratic living" was added, and references to "nonprofit groups" and "admission fee" were deleted. The resulting article broadened the sense of the original by stating that library meeting rooms be available "on equal terms to all groups in the community regardless of their beliefs or affiliations." As adopted by the ALA Council, the revised "Library's Bill of Rights" read as follows:

Today indications in many parts of the world point to growing intolerance, suppression of free speech, and censorship affecting the rights of minorities and individuals. Mindful of this, the Council of the American Library Association publicly affirms its belief in the following basic policies which should govern the services of free public libraries.

1. Books and other reading matter selected for purchase from the public funds should be chosen because of value and interest to people of the community, and in no case should the selection be influenced by the race or nationality or the political or religious views of the writers.

2. As far as available material permits, all sides of questions on which differences of opinion exist should

be represented fairly and adequately in the books and other reading matter purchased for public use.

3. The library as an institution to educate for democratic living should especially welcome the use of its meeting rooms for socially useful and cultural activities and the discussion of current public questions. Library meeting rooms should be available on equal terms to all groups in the community regardless of their beliefs or affiliations.

The three-point declaration approved by the Council was recommended by the Association to governing boards of individual libraries for adoption. ALA could not force individual librarians and boards to take specific action but this policy statement, as all other Association recommendations and statements, provided a guide.

For five years, the "Library's Bill of Rights" stood without change. In 1944, under the chairmanship of Leon Carnovsky, the Intellectual Freedom Committee recommended that Article 1 of the document be amended to include the statement, "Further, books believed to be factually correct should not be banned or removed from the library simply because they are disapproved of by some people." Approved by the ALA Council on October 14, 1944, the amendment proclaimed for the first time the Association's position regarding the banning or removal of materials. The addition, however, also introduced the phrase "factually correct," which was later to be a source of controversy, debate, and change.

Four years later, under the chairmanship of David K. Berninghausen, the Intellectual Freedom Committee recommended a broad revision of the "Library's Bill of Rights" and called for a considerable expansion of the document's scope. Its introductory passage was pared to a precise statement of the Association's purpose: "The Council of the American Library Association reaffirms its belief in the following basic policies which should govern the services of all libraries." By 1948, there was no longer the pre-World War II need to point out "growing intolerance, suppression of free speech, and censorship affecting the rights of minorities and individuals." In the developing Cold War, those factors justifying the 1939 policy were even more evident, and it was recognized that the remedies stated in the "Library's Bill of Rights" were necessary to protect free library service in times of peace as well as of crisis.

Article 1 was prefaced by the phrase, "As a responsibility of library service." Intellectual freedom was thus clearly related to the process of materials selection, and moreover, highlighted by being designated as a "responsibility." Reference to purchase from the public funds was deleted, thereby extending application of the policy to all library materials, not just those acquired through purchase. Whereas the 1939 document stated that selection should not be influenced by the race, nationality, or political or religious views of writers, the revision more explicitly said that no materials by any authors should be excluded on those grounds.

The first part of Article 2 was changed to effect a smoother reading, but there were no substantive alterations. However, the 1944 amendment concerning "books believed to be factually correct" was changed to "books . . . of sound factual authority" and the word "banned" was replaced by "proscribed." Despite their seeming slightness, these subtle changes in the second part of the article actually enlarged the scope of the policy.

A totally new Article 3 recognized the need of libraries to challenge "censorship of books, urged or practiced by volunteer arbiters of morals or political opinion or by organizations that would establish a coercive concept of Americanism." A new Article 4 recognized the libraries' responsibility to cooperate with "allied groups . . . in science, education, and book publishing in resisting all abridgment of the free access to ideas and full freedom of expression." Article 3 of the 1939 document, concerning the use of library meeting rooms, became Article 5 of the new policy. Although the wording was altered, no change was made in the intent.

The entire recommended revision was adopted by the ALA Council on June 18, 1948. In effect, it was a completely different document from its predecessor, the 1939 bill. The new bill's scope and possible applications were broadly expanded establishing its national significance. For the first time, the policy mentioned censorship and also for the first time, the Association declared the responsibility of libraries to challenge censorship—alone and with allied organizations. As adopted by the Council, the newly entitled "Library Bill of Rights" read as follows:

> The Council of the American Library Association reaffirms its belief in the following basic policies which should govern the services of all libraries.

1. As a responsibility of library service, books and other reading matter selected should be chosen for values of interest, information and enlightenment of all the people of the community. In no case should any material be excluded because of race or nationality, or the political or religious views of the writer.

2. There should be the fullest practicable provision of material presenting all points of view concerning the problems and issues of our times, international, national, and local; and books or other reading matter of sound factual authority should not be proscribed or removed from library shelves because of partisan or doctrinal disapproval.

3. Censorship of books, urged or practiced by volunteer arbiters of morals or political opinion or by organizations that would establish a coercive concept of Americanism, must be challenged by libraries in maintenance of their responsibility to provide public information and enlightenment through the printed word.

4. Libraries should enlist the cooperation of allied groups in the fields of science, of education, and of book publishing in resisting all abridgment of the free access to ideas and full freedom of expression that are the tradition and heritage of Americans.

5. As an institution of education for democratic living, the library should welcome the use of its meeting rooms for socially useful and cultural activities and discussion of current public questions. Such meeting places should be available on equal terms to all groups in the community regardless of the beliefs and affiliations of their members.

While the text of the 1948 document remained unchanged until 1961, its application was broadened in 1951. On the recommendation of the Intellectual Freedom Committee, with the endorsement of the Audio-Visual Board, the Council unanimously resolved that "the Library Bill of Rights shall be interpreted as applying to all materials and media of communication used or collected by libraries." The statement, appended as a footnote to all printings of the "Library Bill of Rights" until June 27, 1967, resulted from a Peoria, Illinois, case of attempted censorship by the American Legion and a local newspaper. The Peoria Public Library was pressured to remove the films *The Brotherhood of Man, Boundary Lines*, and *Peoples of the U.S.S.R.* All three films appeared on the ALA Audio-Visual Committee's 1947 list of films suggested for purchase by small libraries. The Educational Film Library Association urged ALA to combat censorship of library film collections, but some librarians contended that the "Library Bill of Rights" applied only to print on paper. The Council resolved the problem by its action of February 3, 1951.

In 1961, another major addition to the "Library Bill of Rights" was approved by the Council. From 1948 through February 1961, the library profession had studied the problem of segregation in libraries. A study made by the Association's Special Committee on Civil Liberties recommended that a new article be added to the "Library Bill of Rights" stating that "the rights of an individual to the use of a library should not be denied or abridged because of his race, religion, national origins or political views." The recommendation was approved by the Council February 2, 1961. The new statement became Article 5 and the old Article 5, concerning use of meeting rooms, became Article 6. The revised "Library Bill of Rights" read:

> The Council of the American Library Association reaffirms its belief in the following basic policies which should govern the services of all libraries.
>
> 1. As a responsibility of library service, books and other reading matter selected should be chosen for values of interest, information and enlightenment of all the people of the community. In no case should any book be excluded because of the race or nationality or the political or religious views of the writer.
>
> 2. There should be the fullest practicable provision of material presenting all points of view concerning the problems and issues of our times, international, national, and local; and books or other reading matter of sound factual authority should not be proscribed or removed from library shelves because of partisan or doctrinal disapproval.
>
> 3. Censorship of books, urged or practiced by volunteer arbiters of morals or political opinion or by organizations that would establish a coercive concept of Americanism, must be challenged by libraries in maintenance of their responsibility to provide public information and enlightenment through the printed word.
>
> 4. Libraries should enlist the cooperation of allied groups in the fields of science, of education, and of book publishing in resisting all abridgment of the free

access to ideas and full freedom of expression that are the tradition and heritage of Americans.

5. The rights of an individual to the use of a library should not be denied or abridged because of his race, religion, national origins or political views.

6. As an institution of education for democratic living, the library should welcome the use of its meeting rooms for socially useful and cultural activities and discussion of current public questions. Such meeting places should be available on equal terms to all groups in the community regardless of the beliefs and affiliations of their members.

By official action of the Council on February 3, 1951, the "Library Bill of Rights" shall be interpreted to apply to all materials and media of communication used or collected by libraries.

On June 27, 1967, almost thirty years after its origin, the "Library Bill of Rights" underwent its second thorough revision. The need for change was made explicit during a special preconference, sponsored by the Intellectual Freedom Committee under the chairmanship of Ervin Gaines, held prior to the 1965 Midwinter Meeting in Washington, D.C. The primary target in the text was the phrase "of sound factual authority," introduced into Article 1 in 1944, and revised and transferred to Article 2 in 1948. Criticism of the phrase arose when a librarian in Belleville, Illinois, used it to exclude a Protestant publication which he, being Catholic, described as lacking "sound factual authority."

In their discussion of the Belleville situation, the preconference participants determined that some of the most profound and influential publications in our culture lack the element of "sound factual authority," and the phrase itself could easily be abused to thwart the intent and purpose of the "Library Bill of Rights." It was apparent that the phrase also effectively held the Association from defending fiction or any of those great works which start from philosophical premises having nothing to do with fact.

Along with a recommendation that the troublesome phrase be dropped, the Intellectual Freedom Committee also asked that several other textual changes be made. In Articles 1 and 5, the word "social" was a suggested addition because of far-reaching results of the civil rights movement. In Article 4, the Committee recommended eliminating the phrase "that are the tradition and heritage of Americans" because it was both redundant and nationalistic. The Committee further recommended that the reference in Article 4 be expanded beyond the groups in science, education, and book publishing the reflect the wider context in which librarians and the Association actually operated.

It was also recommended that Article 6, concerning the use of meeting rooms, be amended to include the phrase, "provided that the meetings be open to the public." This amendment clarified the Association's position regarding the use of library meeting rooms by private groups with restricted attendance. The enlarged scope of the text led the Committee to recommend that "library materials" be substituted for "reading matter," thus making the footnote of 1951 regarding nonprint materials unnecessary.

By the time the Intellectual Freedom Committee's proposed changes came before the Council in 1967, a preconference on Intellectual Freedom and the Teenager had recommended that young people be given free access to all books in a library collection. Accordingly, the Committee included with its previous suggestions the recommendation that Article 5 include the word "age."

On June 28, 1967, the Council adopted all of the Committee's recommendations. The resulting document constitutes the present "Library Bill of Rights." In its current form, the "Library Bill of Rights" presents a statement very different from its 1939 progenitor. Whereas the original document concerned itself primarily with unbiased book selection, a balanced collection, and open meeting rooms, the present version goes much further. It recognizes that censorship of any materials and in any guise eventually affects the library. The current bill therefore provides libraries with principles for opposing censorship and promoting intellectual freedom, in the broadest senses. Even though it is thoroughly refined, the document is still not above criticism. Some professionals have suggested that the bill ignores sexist discrimination, that it says nothing about institutional censorship in college and research libraries, and that Article 6 involves practice rather than principle. As its history has proved, however, the "Library Bill of Rights" is a viable document.

LIBRARY BILL OF RIGHTS

The Council of the American Library Association reaffirms its belief in the following basic policies which should govern the services of all libraries.

1. As a responsibility of library service, books and other library materials selected should be chosen for values of interest, information and enlightenment of all the people of the community. In no case should library materials be excluded because of the race or nationality or the social, political, or religious views of the authors.

2. Libraries should provide books and other materials presenting all points of view concerning the problems and issues of our times; no library materials should be proscribed or removed from libraries because of partisan or doctrinal disapproval.

3. Censorship should be challenged by libraries in the maintenance of their responsibility to provide public information and enlightenment.

4. Libraries should cooperate with all persons and groups concerned with resisting abridgment of free expression and free access to ideas.

5. The rights of an individual to the use of a library should not be denied or abridged because of his age, race, religion, national origins or social or political views.

6. As an institution of education for democratic living, the library should welcome the use of its meeting rooms for socially useful and cultural activities and discussion of current public questions. Such meeting places should be available on equal terms to all groups in the community regardless of the beliefs and affiliations of their members, provided that the meetings be open to the public.

Adopted June 18, 1948. Amended February 2, 1961, and June 27, 1967, by the ALA Council.

Declaración de Derechos Para las Bibliotecas

El Concilio de la American Library Association reafirma su creencia en las siguientes declaraciones básicas, las cuales deben de gobernar a los servicios de todas las bibliotecas.

1. Como responsabilidad de servicio bibliotecario, libros y otras materias deben de seleccionarse por valores de interés, información e instrucción en beneficio de toda la comunidad. En ningun caso deben de excluirse las materias bibliotecarias por razones de raza o nacionalidad o a causa del punto de vista social, político o religioso de los autores.

2. Todas las bibliotecas deben de ofrecer libros y otras materias que representen todos los puntos de vista relacionados a los problemas y preocupaciones de nuestros tiempos; ninguna materia bibliotecaria debe de proscribirse o de removerse de una biblioteca por razón de desaprobación partidaria o doctrinal.

3. Las bibliotecas deben de desafiar a la censura para mantener su responsabilidad de proveer información pública e instructiva.

4. Las bibliotecas deben de cooperar con toda persona y con todo grupo dedicados a resistir la privación de la expresión libre y el libre acceso a todas ideas.

5. Los derechos de un individuo al uso de una biblioteca no deben de ser negados o privados por razones de edad, raza, religión, orígenes nacionales o creencias sociales o políticas.

6. Como institución de educación para la vida democrática, la biblioteca debe de fomentar el uso de sus facilidades de reunión para actos culturales y constructivamente sociales, y para la discusión de cuestiones públicas corrientes. Tales sitios de reunión deben de disponerse igualmente a todos los grupos de la comunidad no obstante las creencias y afiliaciones de sus miembros, siempre que las reuniones sean abiertas al público.

Adoptado el 18 de junio de 1948. Enmendado el 2 de febrero de 1961, y el 27 de junio de 1967 por el Concilio de la American Library Association.

Translated by Cynthia Baird, Gladis M. Carballo, Eddie Razo, Keith Revelle, and Raquel Torres N.—Latin American Library of the Oakland Public Library.

Interpretations of the "Library Bill of Rights"

Although the articles of the "Library Bill of Rights" are unambiguous statements of basic principles which should govern the service of all libraries, questions do arise concerning application of these principles to specific library practices. For example, a 1951 Peoria, Illinois, case involving certain films in the public library required the Association to clarify the application of the "Library Bill of Rights" to nonprint materials. A recommendation by the Intellectual Freedom Committee and the Audio-Visual Board resulted in the ALA Council's adding an interpretive footnote, explaining that the "Library Bill of Rights" applies to all materials and media of communication used or collected by libraries.

During the 1971 Annual Conference in Dallas, the Intellectual Freedom Committee considered censorship cases which clearly called for interpretations of the "Library Bill of Rights" to define its application to certain practices. Believing that frequent revisions, amendments, or additions of footnotes weaken the document's effectiveness, the Committee resolved instead to develop statements to be called "Interpretations of the 'Library Bill of Rights.'" The Committee said further that certain documents already in existence should be designated as Interpretations of the "Library Bill of Rights."

Following are those documents designated by the Intellectual Freedom Committee as Interpretations of the "Library Bill of Rights" and background statements detailing the philosophy and history of each. These documents are policies of the American Library Association, having been adopted by the ALA Council.

Free Access to Libraries for Minors

The question of whether or not intellectual freedom in libraries applies to children and young adults has been debated by librarians since the early years of the profession's involvement with intellectual freedom. The question was considered many times by the Intellectual Freedom Committee, and led to the preconference institute on Intellectual Freedom and the Teenager, held in San Francisco, June 23–25, 1967.

Sponsored jointly by the Intellectual Freedom Committee, the Young Adult Services Division, and the American Association of School Librarians, and attended by approximately 400 librarians, the preconference featured a variety of speakers of national reputation, including author Kenneth Rexroth, attorneys Stanley Fleishman and Alex P. Allain, book review editor Robert Kirsh, and library young adult consultant Esther Helfand. The most outspoken panelist was Dr. Edgar L. Freidenberg, author of *Coming of Age in America*, who told participants:

> The library is just one more place where the kids are taught they are second-class citizens. They learn this not only from the books pressed upon them by the helpful librarian but even more so from the very atmosphere of the place.[1]

In his summary of the three-day meeting, IFC Chairman Ervin Gaines dwelt at length on Freidenberg's comments, saying:

> He made the assumption that intellectual freedom was an inalienable right and that age is not a morally relevant factor and that adults have themselves no right to determine for youth access to ideas. This assumption which came at the very beginning of his talk echoed and re-echoed throughout the conference. There was surprising unanimity of opinion on this particular point.[2]

1. *San Francisco Examiner & Chronicle* June 25, 1967.
2. *Newsletter on Intellectual Freedom* 16:54 (Sept. 1967).

As the preconference progressed, there was also surprising unanimity that not only teenagers were the focus of the discussions, but all young people. This was reflected in one of the major recommendations of the institute, "that free access to all books in a library collection be granted to young people."[3]

Later, during the 1967 Annual Conference, Mr. Gaines moved that the Council adopt a revised version of the "Library Bill of Rights." He introduced his motion with the following remarks:

> At a meeting of the Intellectual Freedom Committee yesterday two minor amendments were suggested to this text [the revised "Library Bill of Rights"]. In section 5 we suggest that the word "age" be inserted. . . . This suggestion comes as a result of recommendations from the preconference on "Intellectual Freedom and the Teenager" which was held last week.

The change was approved by the Council, and the Association, well in advance of society in general, took a significant stand, approving free access for minors to all the materials in a library collection.

After 1967, the word "age" in the "Library Bill of Rights" was a constant source of confusion. Did it mean children should be able to take home any materials in a library collection or were some restrictions permissible? What about double card systems or multiple card systems, restricting minors to use of only part of the collection? These and other questions accrued until the IFC's 1972 Midwinter Meeting. Twenty hours of meetings were dominated by discussions of minors and library access problems, all related to the word "age" in the "Library Bill of Rights."

After the meeting, the Committee announced plans to develop a position statement concerning access to libraries for minors. A draft was subsequently sent, in the spring of 1972, to the boards of the Public Library Association, the American Association of School Librarians, the Children's Services Division, the Young Adult Services Division, and the American Library Trustee Association. At its annual meeting in June 1972, the IFC approved the statement and recommended it to the ALA Council who adopted it on June 30, 1972, as an ALA policy entitled "Free Access to Libraries for Minors."

3. Ibid., p.55.

FREE ACCESS TO LIBRARIES FOR MINORS

An Interpretation of the "Library Bill of Rights"

Some library procedures and practices effectively deny minors access to certain services and materials available to adults. Such procedures and practices are not in accord with the "Library Bill of Rights" and are opposed by the American Library Association.

Restrictions take a variety of forms, including, among others, restricted reading rooms for adult use only, library cards limiting circulation of some materials to adults only, closed collections for adult use only, and interlibrary loan service for adult use only.

All limitations in minors' access to library materials and services violate Article 5 of the "Library Bill of Rights," which states, "The rights of an individual to the use of a library should not be denied or abridged because of his age. . . . " Limiting access to some services and materials to only adults abridges the use of libraries for minors. "Use of the library" includes use of, and access to, all library materials and services.

Restrictions are often initiated under the assumption that certain materials are "harmful" to minors, or in an effort to avoid controversy with parents who might think so. The librarian who would restrict the access of minors to materials and services because of actual or suspected parental objection should bear in mind that he is not *in loco parentis* in his position as librarian. Individual intellectual levels and family backgrounds are significant factors not accommodated by a uniform policy based upon age.

In today's world, children are exposed to adult life much earlier than in the past. They read materials and view a variety of media on the adult level at home and elsewhere.

Approved June 30, 1972, by the ALA Council.

16

Current emphasis upon early childhood education has also increased opportunities for young people to learn and to have access to materials, and has decreased the validity of using chronological age as an index to the use of libraries. The period of time during which children are interested in reading materials specifically designed for them grows steadily shorter, and librarians must recognize and adjust to this change if they wish to maintain the patronage of young people.

The American Library Association holds that it is the parent—and only the parent—who may restrict his children—and only *his* children—from access to library materials and services. The parent who would rather his child did not have access to certain materials should so advise the child.

The word "age" was incorporated into Article 5 of the "Library Bill of Rights" as a direct result of a preconference entitled "Intellectual Freedom and the Teenager," held in San Francisco in June 1967. One recommendation of the preconference participants was "that free access to all books in a library collection be granted to young people." The preconference generally concluded that young people are entitled to the same access to libraries and to the materials in libraries as are adults and that materials selection should not be diluted on that account.

This does not mean, for instance, that issuing different types of borrowers' cards to minors and adults is, *per se*, contrary to the "Library Bill of Rights." If such practices are used for purposes of gathering statistics, the various kinds of cards carry no implicit or explicit limitations on access to materials and services. Neither does it mean that maintaining separate children's collections is a violation of the "Library Bill of Rights," provided that no patron is restricted to the use of only certain collections.

The Association's position does not preclude isolating certain materials for legitimate protection of irreplaceable or very costly works from careless use. Such "restricted-use" areas as rare book rooms are appropriate if the materials so classified are genuinely rare, and not merely controversial.

Unrestrictive selection policies, developed with care for principles of intellectual freedom and the "Library Bill of Rights," should not be vitiated by administrative practices which restrict minors to the use of only part of a library's collections and services.

17

Statement on Labeling

In late 1950, the Intellectual Freedom Committee received a report that the Montclair, New Jersey, chapter of the Sons of the American Revolution (SAR) was exerting pressure on New Jersey libraries to put a prominent label or inscription on "publications which advocate or favor communism, or which are issued or distributed by any communist organization or any other organization formally designated by any authorized government official or agency as communistic or subversive. . . . " The SAR said further that such publications "should not be freely available in libraries to readers or in schools to pupils, but should be obtainable only by signing suitable applications."[1]

Rutherford D. Rogers, chairman of the IFC, reported the matter to the ALA Council on July 13, 1951, and said groups other than the SAR have tried to use such labeling as a means of limiting the freedom to read. He cited religious groups which sometimes asked libraries to label "objectionable" publications, and mentioned that other "patriotic" organizations were moving toward similar proposals. Mr. Rogers also reported that in April 1951 the Association received a letter from the Montclair chapter of the SAR requesting ALA to adopt a policy advocating that communistic and subversive materials not only be labeled but also be segregated from other materials in the library collection and given out only upon written and signed application.

The Intellectual Freedom Committee believed such practices violated intellectual freedom principles and the labeling of books by points of view should not be undertaken by any library. The Committee also noted that it was not clear who would do such labeling, who would decide what is communistic or subversive, or by what criteria such decisions would be made. In addition, the process was envisioned as expensive and time consuming, involving examination of all materials in a library collection. The impracticality and financial problems of such a project, however, were not deemed

1. *ALA Bulletin* 45:241 (July/Aug. 1951).

relevant to the Association's policy concerning the practice. As Mr. Rogers pointed out, policy was to be based on the principle involved.

The IFC's study of the SAR proposal resulted in a six-point statement. Before presenting the statement to the Council for adoption as an ALA policy, the Committee conducted an informal survey of twenty-four libraries around the country. Twenty responded, all agreeing that labeling violated basic principles of intellectual freedom and should not be practiced by libraries. The IFC's six-point "Statement on Labeling" was approved by the Council as an ALA policy on July 13, 1951:

> 1. Although totalitarian states find it easy and even proper, according to their ethics, to establish criteria for judging publications as "subversive," injustice and ignorance rather than justice and enlightenment result from such practices, and the American Library Association has a responsibility to take a stand against the establishment of such criteria in a democratic state.
>
> 2. Libraries do not advocate the ideas found in their collections. The presence of a magazine or book in a library does not indicate an endorsement of its contents by the library.
>
> 3. No one person should take the responsibility of labeling publications. No sizeable group of persons would be likely to agree either on the types of materials which should be labeled or the sources of information which should be regarded with suspicion. As a practical consideration, a librarian who labeled a book or magazine pro-communist might be sued for libel.
>
> 4. Labeling is an attempt to prejudice the reader, and as such, it is a censor's tool.
>
> 5. Labeling violates the spirit of the "Library Bill of Rights."
>
> 6. Although we are all agreed that communism is a threat to the free world, if materials are labeled to pacify one group, there is no excuse for refusing to label any item in the library's collection. Because communism, fascism, or other authoritarianisms tend to suppress ideas and attempt to coerce individuals to conform to a specific ideology, American librarians must be opposed to such "isms." We are, then, anti-

communist, but we are also opposed to any other group which aims at closing any path to knowledge.

The 1951 "Statement on Labeling" was adopted as policy by many libraries, and over the years was a useful tool in combatting this brand of censorship. One incident involving attempts to label library materials occurred at the St. Charles County Library, St. Charles, Missouri, in 1968 and concluded with a unique twist. The case began when Mrs. Nina S. Ladof, the librarian, was presented with a petition requesting the removal of *Ramparts* magazine. The library dismissed the petition, explaining that *Ramparts* was purchased in accordance with the library's book selection policy, which included the "Library Bill of Rights" and "The Freedom to Read."

After the initial attempt to remove *Ramparts*, several months passed. Eventually, though, the original complainant presented the librarian with a sheaf of petitions from the Veterans of Foreign Wars, the American Legion, the Lions Club, and a church. With variations, the petitions read:

> We, the undersigned, do hereby petition the Library Board of the County of St. Charles, requesting that any book or publication on file in the St. Charles County Library System authored, published, or edited by any individual or group of individuals having been cited by any official Federal or State UnAmerican Activities Committee or Fact-Finding Committee as subversive or unAmerican in nature or belonging to any organization having been cited as subversive or unAmerican, be so explicitly labeled in a conspicuous manner for the information of the patrons of the St. Charles County Libraries.

Mrs. Ladof pointed out that Dr. Benjamin Spock, author of *The Common Sense of Baby Care*, was sentenced on charges of aiding young men to avoid military service. Would this book require a label? Pursuing this example further, Mrs. Ladof wrote to Spock's publishers to ask what action they would take if she did, in fact, affix a label to his works. Two replied that they would consider it possible grounds for legal action against the library. Dr. Spock's own attorney concurred.

Both the American Civil Liberties Union and the Freedom of Information Center at the University of Missouri provided Mrs. Ladof with the legal opinion that labeling a work, as requested in the petition, would be grounds for a libel action by the author whose works were involved because of the injury to the sale of his works that might result. Even if the label were factual, such as "so-and-so was a member of the Communist Party in 1941," he would have grounds to prove such injury. In fact, injury need not actually occur; it need only be a possibility for a court to award substantial damages to a plaintiff in such a case. And, since library boards of trustees cannot be sued as a body, each member would be liable for the damages awarded.

Armed with this information, and with the board's unanimous belief that labels are forms of censorship, and, as such, completely opposed to basic library policies, the library issued a firm statement rejecting the proposed labeling. The statement included information from legal sources and paraphrased and expanded the six points of the ALA "Statement on Labeling." All persons interested in the matter were sent copies with an explanatory letter. *Ramparts* and other literature written by so-called subversives continued to circulate unlabeled.

The 1951 "Statement on Labeling" stood without revision until 1971. At that time, study of the policy confirmed that some sections were framed in a language which reflected the Association's response to a specific threat—the labeling of "subversive" or "communist" materials. The Intellectual Freedom Committee concluded that, while these sections once met a particular need, they limited the document's usefulness.

To make the "Statement on Labeling" applicable to a broader range of labeling problems, even encompassing "harmful matter," the Intellectual Freedom Committee recommended a revised version to the Council. The 1971 revision was designated an "Interpretation of the 'Library Bill of Rights'" to emphasize the relationship between Articles 1, 2, and 3 of that document and the "Statement on Labeling." The revision was adopted by the Council on June 25, 1971.

STATEMENT ON LABELING
An Interpretation of the "Library Bill of Rights"

Because labeling violates the spirit of the "Library Bill of Rights," the American Library Association opposes the technique of labeling as a means of predisposing readers against library materials for the following reasons:

1. Labeling* is an attempt to prejudice the reader, and as such it is a censor's tool.

2. Although some find it easy and even proper, according to their ethics, to establish criteria for judging publications as objectionable, injustice and ignorance rather than justice and enlightenment result from such practices, and the American Library Association must oppose the establishment of such criteria.

3. Libraries do not advocate the ideas found in their collections. The presence of a magazine or book in a library does not indicate an endorsement of its contents by the library.

4. No one person should take the responsibility of labeling publications. No sizeable group of persons would be likely to agree either on the types of material which should be labeled or the sources of information which should be regarded with suspicion. As a practical consideration, a librarian who labels a book or magazine might be sued for libel.

5. If materials are labeled to pacify one group, there is no excuse for refusing to label any item in the library's collection. Because authoritarians tend to suppress ideas and attempt to coerce individuals to conform to a specific ideology, the American Library Association opposes such efforts which aim at closing any path to knowledge.

* "Labeling," as it is referred to in the "Statement on Labeling," is the practice of describing or designating certain library materials, by affixing a prejudicial label to them or segregating them by a prejudicial system, so as to predispose readers against the materials.
Adopted July 13, 1951. Amended June 25, 1971, by the ALA Council.

Expurgation of Library Materials

The December 1971 issue of *School Library Journal* (p.7) carried the following report submitted by one of its readers:

> Maurice Sendak might faint but a staff member of Caldwell Parish Library [Louisiana], knowing that the patrons of the community might object to the illustrations in *In the Night Kitchen*, solved the problem by diapering the little boys with white tempera paint. Other libraries might wish to do the same.

In response, Ursula Nordstrom, publisher of Harper Junior Books, sent a statement to over 380 librarians, professors, publishers, authors, and artists throughout the United States:

> [The news item sent to *School Library Journal*] is representative of several such reports about Maurice Sendak's *In the Night Kitchen*, a book for children, that have come out of public and school libraries throughout the country.
>
> At first, the thought of librarians painting diapers or pants on the naked hero of Sendak's book might seem amusing, merely a harmless eccentricity on the part of some prim few. On reconsideration, however, this behavior should be recognized for what it is: an act of censorship by mutilation rather than by obvious suppression.

Over 425 persons signed the statement of protest circulated by Miss Nordstrom.

The expurgation of *In the Night Kitchen* was brought to the attention of the Intellectual Freedom Committee by the Children's Book Council in June 1972. During its meeting at the 1972 ALA Annual Conference in Chicago, the Committee decided, after considering whether expurgation was already covered by the "Library Bill of Rights," that a statement should be issued specifically on expurgation. During the 1973 Midwinter Meeting in Washington, D.C., the Committee approved the present statement on expurgation of library materials and sent it to the ALA Council for approval. The statement was adopted by the Council as an ALA policy on February 2, 1973.

EXPURGATION OF LIBRARY MATERIALS

An Interpretation of the "Library Bill of Rights"

Library materials are chosen for their value and interest to the community the library serves. If library materials were acquired for these reasons and in accordance with a written statement on materials selection, then to expurgate must be interpreted as a violation of the "Library Bill of Rights." For purposes of this statement, expurgation includes deletion, excision, alteration or obliteration. By such expurgation, the library is in effect denying access to the complete work and the full ideas that the work was intended to express; such action stands in violation of Article 2 of the "Library Bill of Rights," which states that "no library materials should be proscribed or removed from libraries because of partisan or doctrinal disapproval."

The act of expurgation has serious implications. It involves a determination by an individual that it is necessary to restrict the availability of that material. It is, in fact, censorship.

When a work is expurgated, under the assumption that certain sections of that work would be harmful to minors, the situation is no less serious. Expurgation of any library materials imposes a restriction, without regard to the rights and desires of all library users.

Adopted February 2, 1973, by the ALA Council.

Sexism, Racism, and Other -isms in Library Materials

During the 1971 Midwinter Meeting in Los Angeles, the ALA Intellectual Freedom Committee met with representatives of the International Conference of Police Associations' Executive Board. The meeting was to provide a forum for discussing police efforts to remove William Steig's *Sylvester and the Magic Pebble* from public and school libraries. During the meeting, the officers raised a provocative and embarrassing questions for librarians. They asked why some librarians were quick to comply with requests to remove another children's book, *Little Black Sambo*, from their collections when blacks complained that its illustrations were degrading; yet now, when police officers found William Steig's pigs dressed as law enforcement officers to be degrading, librarians objected vociferously to taking the book out of their collections.

The evasive response from the IFC was generally to the effect that the Committee had difficulties impressing upon members of the library profession the importance of the principles of intellectual freedom. The inability to answer the officers' charge adequately acknowledged the accusation implicit in the question: Some librarians do employ a double standard when it comes to their practice of intellectual freedom and their commitment to it. Many librarians express a strong commitment to the principles of intellectual freedom, but fail to grasp that the concept of intellectual freedom, in its pure sense, promotes no causes, furthers no movement, and favors no viewpoints. *Little Black Sambo* and *Sylvester and the Magic Pebble* did not bring new issues before the library profession. These books only inherited the cloak of controversy that had already surrounded such diverse works as *Huckleberry Finn*, *Mother Goose Nursery Rhymes and Fairy Tales*, *Doctor Doolittle*, and *The Merchant of Venice*.

Article 2 of the "Library Bill of Rights" states that "no library materials should be proscribed or removed from libraries because of partisan or doctrinal disapproval" (pt.1, p.11). The phrase "no library materials" does not appear by accident. Before June 1967, the sentence concluded, "books or other reading matter of sound factual authority should not be proscribed or removed from library shelves because of partisan or doctrinal disapproval" (pt.1, p.7). Article 2 was revised in 1967 because some librarians used alleged lack of "sound factual authority" as a basis for removing library materials. To determine which materials lacked "sound factual authority," many deferred to their personal conceptions of "fact" and "authority." One of the most extreme examples, cited at the time of the revision, was of a Catholic librarian who excluded Protestant publications because they were not of "sound factual authority." Today, the simpler, broader phrase "no library materials" in the "Library Bill of Rights" leaves no room for interpretation. The revised statement reflects the philosophy that freedom is indivisible, and that tolerance, if it is to be meaningful, must be tolerance for all points of view.

At the 1972 Midwinter Meeting in Chicago, the Intellectual Freedom Committee reported its intention to prepare a statement making clear the meaning of the "Library Bill of Rights" as it pertains to attempts to censor library materials because of alleged racism, sexism, or any other "isms." The statement was approved by the IFC on June 25, 1972. It was subsequently submitted to the ALA Council at the 1973 Midwinter Meeting in Washington, D.C., and approved as an ALA policy on February 2, 1973.

SEXISM, RACISM, AND OTHER -ISMS IN LIBRARY MATERIALS

An Interpretation of the "Library Bill of Rights"

Traditional aims of censorship efforts have been to suppress political, sexual, or religious expressions. The same three subjects have also been the source of most complaints about materials in library collections. Another basis for complaints, however, has become more and more frequent. Due, perhaps, to increased awareness of the rights of minorities and increased efforts to secure those rights, libraries are being asked to remove, restrict or reconsider some materials which are allegedly derogatory to specific minorities or which supposedly perpetuate stereotypes and false images of minorities. Among the several recurring "isms" used to describe the contents of the materials objected to are "racism" and "sexism."

Complaints that library materials convey a derogatory or false image of a minority strike the personal social consciousness and sense of responsibility of some librarians who—accordingly—comply with the requests to remove such materials. While such efforts to counteract injustices are understandable, and perhaps even commendable as reflections of deep personal commitments to the ideal of equality for all people, they are—nonetheless—in conflict with the professional responsibility of librarians to guard against encroachments upon intellectual freedom.

This responsibility has been espoused and reaffirmed by the American Library Association in many of its basic documents on intellectual freedom over the past thirty years. The most concise statement of the Association's position appears in Article 2 of the "Library Bill of Rights," which states that "Libraries should provide books and materials presenting all points of view concerning the problems and issues of our

Adopted February 2, 1973, by the ALA Council.

27

times; no library materials should be proscribed or removed because of partisan or doctrinal disapproval."

While the application of this philosophy may seem simple when dealing with political, religious, or even sexual expressions, its full implications become somewhat difficult when dealing with ideas, such as racism or sexism, which many find abhorrent, repugnant and inhumane. But, as stated in "The Freedom to Read":

> It is inevitable in the give and take of the democratic process that the political, the moral, or the aesthetic concepts of an individual or group will occasionally collide with those of another individual or group. In a free society each individual is free to determine for himself what he wishes to read, and each group is free to determine what it will recommend to its freely associated members. But no group has the right to take the law into its own hands, and to impose its own concept of politics or morality upon other members of a democratic society. Freedom is no freedom if it is accorded only to the accepted and the inoffensive. . . . We realize that the application of these propositions may mean the dissemination of ideas and manners of expression that are repugnant to many persons. We do not state these propositions in the comfortable belief that what people read is unimportant. We believe rather that what people read is deeply important; that ideas can be dangerous; but that the suppression of ideas is fatal to a democratic society. Freedom itself is a dangerous way of life, but it is ours.

Some find this creed acceptable when dealing with materials for adults but cannot extend its application to materials for children. Such reluctance is generally based on the belief that children are more susceptible to being permanently influenced—even damaged—by objectionable materials than are adults. The "Library Bill of Rights," however, makes no distinction between materials and services for children and adults. Its principles of free access to all materials available apply to every person; as stated in Article 5, "The rights of an individual to the use of a library should not be denied or abridged because of his age, race, religion, national origins or social or political views."

Some librarians deal with the problem of objectionable materials by labeling them or listing them as "racist" or "sexist." This kind of action, too, has long been opposed by the American Library Association through its "Statement on Labeling," which says,

> If materials are labeled to pacify one group, there is no excuse for refusing to label any item in the library's collection. Because authoritarians tend to suppress ideas and attempt to coerce individuals to conform to a specific ideology, the American Library Association opposes such efforts which aim at closing any path to knowledge.

Others deal with the problem of objectionable materials by instituting restrictive circulation or relegating materials to closed or restricted collections. This practice, too, is in violation of the "Library Bill of Rights" as explained in "Restricted Access to Library Materials," which says,

> Too often only "controversial" materials are the subject of such segregation, leading to the conclusion that factors other than theft and mutilation were the true considerations. The distinction is extremely difficult to make, both for the librarian and the patron. Selection policies, carefully developed on the basis of principles of intellectual freedom and the "Library Bill of Rights," should not be vitiated by administrative practices such as restricted access.

The American Library Association has made clear its position concerning the removal of library materials because of partisan or doctrinal disapproval, or because of pressures from interest groups, in another policy statement, the "Resolution on Challenged Materials":

> The American Library Association declares as a matter of firm principle that no challenged material should be removed from any library under any legal or extra-legal pressure, save after an independent determination by a judicial officer in a court of competent jurisdiction and only after an adversary hearing, in accordance with well-established principles of law.

Intellectual freedom, in its purest sense, promotes no causes, furthers no movements, and favors no viewpoints. It only provides for free access to all ideas through which any and all sides of causes and movements may be expressed, discussed, and argued. The librarian cannot let his own preferences limit his degree of tolerance, for freedom is indivisible. Toleration is meaningless without toleration for the detestable.

Reevaluating Library Collections

In both theory and practice, library collections undergo continual reevaluation to ensure that they fulfill and remain responsive to the goals of the institution and the needs of library patrons. The reevaluation process, however, can also be used to achieve the purposes of the censor, purposes manifestly inconsistent with Articles 1 and 2 of the "Library Bill of Rights."

At the 1972 Midwinter Meeting in Chicago, the Intellectual Freedom Committee realized the necessity of an interpretation of the "Library Bill of Rights" with regard to the more general issues involved in reevaluating library collections. (See Sexism, Racism, and Other -isms in Library Materials, pt.1, p.25–29.) Accordingly, the Committee announced its intent to prepare a statement on reevaluation. The document was approved by the Intellectual Freedom Committee at the 1972 Annual Conference in Chicago. It was submitted to the ALA Council at the 1973 Midwinter Meeting in Washington, D.C., and was adopted on February 2, 1973.

REEVALUATING LIBRARY COLLECTIONS

An Interpretation of the "Library Bill of Rights"

The continuous review of library collections to remove physically deteriorated or obsolete materials is one means to maintain active library collections of current interest to users.* Continued reevaluation is closely related to the goals and responsibilities of libraries and is a valuable tool of collection building. This procedure, however, is sometimes used as a convenient means to remove materials thought to be too controversial or disapproved of by segments of the community. Such abuse of the reevaluation function violates the principles of intellectual freedom and is in opposition to Articles 1 and 2 of the "Library Bill of Rights," which state that:

> As a responsibility of library service, books and other library materials selected should be chosen for values of interest, information and enlightenment of all the people of the community. In no case should library materials be excluded because of the race or nationality or the social, political, or religious views of the authors.

> Libraries should provide books and other materials presenting all points of view concerning the problems and issues of our times; no library materials should be proscribed or removed from libraries because of partisan or doctrinal disapproval.

The American Library Association opposes such "silent censorship," and recommends that libraries adopt guidelines setting forth the positive purposes and principles for reevaluation of materials in library collections.

* The traditional term "weeding," implying "the removal of a noxious growth," is purposely avoided because of the imprecise nature of the term.

Adopted February 2, 1973, by the ALA Council.

How Libraries Can Resist Censorship

The early 1960s saw increased censorship attacks on libraries and strenuous assaults on the freedom to read; "witch hunts" in Georgia, censorship of some best sellers and heated controversy over Henry Miller's *Tropic of Cancer* were prominent during the period. In response to this situation, a group of librarians and publishers met in Washington, D.C., on January 5, 1962, to draft a statement on censorship. The committee was composed of David H. Clift, executive director of the American Library Association; Dan Lacy, managing director of the American Book Publishers Council; Margaret Dudley, executive secretary of the National Book Committee; Emerson Greenaway, chairman of the ALA Legislative Committee; and Archie McNeal, chairman of the ALA Intellectual Freedom Committee. The statement this group wrote, entitled "How Libraries and Schools Can Resist Censorship," gave support and step-by-step guidelines to ways a library can thwart the censor.

In introducing the statement to the ALA Council, Mr. McNeal urged its support, especially in light of the country-wide attempts at censorship. "How Libraries and Schools Can Resist Censorship" was approved unanimously by the ALA Council on February 1, 1962:

> Libraries of all sizes and types have been under increasing pressures from persons who wish to use the library as an instrument of their own tastes and views. Such individuals and groups are demanding the exclusion or removal of books to which they object or the inclusion of a higher proportion of books that support their views. Similar attacks have been made on schools in connection with books used in their programs. In view of this fact, it seems desirable to set forth a few basic principles that may help librarians, trustees, and school administrators in preserving the freedom and professional integrity of their institutions.
>
> The problem differs somewhat between the public library, with a responsibility to the public to present as wide a spectrum of significant reading matter as its budget can afford, and the school library, whose col-

lections are designed to support the educational objectives of the school. In both, however, there is involved the freedom of the school or the library to meet its professional responsibilities to the whole community.

Every library or school should take certain measures to clarify its policies and establish its community relations. These steps should be taken without regard to any attack or prospect of attack. They will put the institution in a firm and clearly defined position if its book policies are ever called into question.

As a normal operating procedure, every library, and the administration responsible for it, should establish certain principles.

1. There should be a definite book selection policy. This should be in written form and approved by the board of trustees, the school board, or other administrative authority. It should be stated clearly and should be understood by members of the staff. This policy should apply to other materials equally, i.e., films, records, magazines, and pamphlets.

2. A file recording the basis for decision should be kept for titles likely to be questioned or apt to be considered controversial.

3. There should be a clearly defined method for handling complaints. Any complaint should be required to be in writing, and the complainant should be identified properly before the complaint is considered. Action should be deferred until full consideration by appropriate administrative authority.

4. There should be continuing efforts to establish lines of communication to assure mutual understanding with civic, religious, educational, and political bodies.

5. Newspapers of the community should be informed of policies governing book selection and use. Purposes and services of the library should be interpreted through a continuing public relations program, as should the use of books in the school.

6. Participation in local civic organizations and in community affairs is desirable. The library and the school are key centers of the community; the librarian and school administrator should be known publicly as community leaders.

If an attack does come, remember the following:

1. Remain calm. Don't confuse noise with substance. Most attacks come from small groups of people

who have little community backing. Time after time the American people have shown that, given the facts, they will back solidly the responsible exercise of professional freedom by teachers and librarians and that they will insist on protecting their own freedom to read. Insist on the deliberate handling of the complaint under previously established rules. Treat complainants with dignity, courtesy, and good humor.

2. Take immediate steps to assure that the full facts surrounding a complaint are known to the administration. The school librarian should go through the principal to the superintendent and the school board; the public librarian, to the board of trustees or to the appropriate community administration official; the college or university librarian, to the president and through him to the board of trustees. Full, written information should be presented, giving the nature of the problem or complaint and identifying the source.

3. Seek the support of the local press immediately. The freedom to read and the freedom of the press go hand in hand.

4. Inform local civic organizations of the facts and enlist their support where possible.

5. Defend the principles of the freedom to read and the professional responsibility of teachers and librarians rather than the individual book. The laws governing obscenity, subversive material, and other questionable matter are subject to interpretation by the courts. The responsibility for removal of any book from public access should rest with this established process. The responsibility for the use of books in the schools must rest with those responsible for the educational objectives being served.

6. The ALA Intellectual Freedom Committee and other appropriate national and state committees concerned with intellectual freedom should be informed of the nature of the problem. Even though each effort at censorship must be met at the local level, there is often value in the support and assistance of agencies outside the area which have no personal involvement. They often can cite parallel cases and suggest methods of meeting an attack. Similar aid in cases affecting the use of books in the schools can be obtained from the Commission on Professional Rights and Responsibilities of the National Education Association.

The 1962 statement on resisting censorship was endorsed by the Adult Education Association Executive Committee, the American Book Publishers Council, the American Civil Liberties Union, the National Book Committee, the National Council of Teachers of English, the National Education Association Commission on Professional Rights and Responsibilities, and the National Education Association Department of Class Room Teachers.

At the 1972 Midwinter Meeting of the Intellectual Freedom Committee, the original statement on resisting censorship was changed. The document was altered to include all types of libraries, not just school and public libraries, and "library materials" was substituted for "books." The new document, "How Libraries Can Resist Censorship," was adopted by the ALA Council on January 28, 1972.

HOW LIBRARIES CAN RESIST CENSORSHIP

An Interpretation of the "Library Bill of Rights"

Libraries of all sizes and types continue to be targets of pressure from groups and individuals who wish to use the library as an instrument of their own tastes and views. The problem differs somewhat between the public library, with a responsibility to present as wide a spectrum of materials as its budget can afford, and the school or academic library, whose collection is designed to support the educational objectives of the institution. Both, however, involve the freedom of the library to meet its professional responsibilities to the whole community.

To combat censorship efforts from groups and individuals, every library should take certain measures to clarify policies and establish community relations. While these steps should be taken regardless of any attack or prospect of attack, they will provide a firm and clearly defined position if selection policies are challenged. As normal operating procedure, each library should:

1. Maintain a definite materials selection policy. It should be in written form and approved by the appropriate regents or other governing authority. It should apply to all library materials equally.

2. Maintain a clearly defined method for handling complaints. Basic requirements should be that the complaint be filed in writing and the complainant be properly identified before his request is considered. Action should be deferred until full consideration by appropriate administrative authority.

3. Maintain lines of communication with civic, religious, educational, and political bodies of the community. Participa-

Adopted February 1, 1962. Revised January 28, 1972, by the ALA Council.

tion in local civic organizations and in community affairs is desirable. Because the library and the school are key centers of the community, the librarian should be known publicly as a community leader.

4. Maintain a vigorous public relations program on behalf of intellectual freedom. Newspapers, radio, and television should be informed of policies governing materials selection and use, and of any special activities pertaining to intellectual freedom.

Adherence to the practices listed above will not preclude confrontations with pressure groups or individuals but may provide a base from which to counter efforts to place restraints on the library. If a confrontation does occur, librarians should remember the following:

1. Remain calm. Don't confuse noise with substance. Require the deliberate handling of the complaint under previously established rules. Treat the group or individual who complains with dignity, courtesy, and good humor. Given the facts, most citizens will support the responsible exercise of professional freedom by teachers and librarians, and will insist on protecting their own freedom to read.

2. Take immediate steps to assure that the full facts surrounding a complaint are known to the administration and the governing authority. The school librarian should go through the principal to the superintendent and the school board; the public librarian, to the board of trustees or to the appropriate governing authority of the community; the college or university librarian, to the president and through him to the board of trustees. Present full, written information giving the nature of the complaint and identifying the source.

3. Seek the support of the local press when appropriate. The freedom to read and freedom of the press go hand in hand.

4. Inform local civic organizations of the facts and enlist their support when appropriate. Meet negative pressure with positive pressure.

5. In most cases, defend the principle of the freedom to read and the professional responsibility of teachers and librarians. Only rarely is it necessary to defend the individual item. Laws governing obscenity, subversive material, and other questionable matter are subject to interpretation by courts. Responsibility for removal of any library materials from public access rests with this established process.

6. Inform the ALA Office for Intellectual Freedom and other appropriate national and state organizations concerned with intellectual freedom of the nature of the problem. Even though censorship must be fought at the local level, there is value in the support and assistance of agencies outside the area which have no personal involvement. They can often cite parallel cases and suggest methods of meeting an attack.

The principles and procedures discussed above apply to all kinds of censorship attacks and are supported by groups such as the National Education Association, the American Civil Liberties Union, and the National Council of Teachers of English, as well as the American Library Association. While the practices provide positive means for preparing for and meeting pressure group complaints, they serve the more general purpose of supporting the "Library Bill of Rights," particularly Article 3, which states that "censorship should be challenged by libraries in the maintenance of their responsibility to provide public information and enlightenment." Adherence to this principle is especially necessary when under pressure.

Resolution on Challenged Materials

Since June 18, 1948, the "Library Bill of Rights" has stated that library materials should not be "excluded because of the race or nationality or the social, political, or religious views of the authors." The document states further that "no library materials should be proscribed or removed from libraries because of partisan or doctrinal disapproval" (pt.1, p.11). Libraries are still pressured, nevertheless, by many groups and individuals to remove certain material because they find its sexual, political, or religious content objectionable.

Particularly when sexually explicit materials are the object of censorship efforts, librarians and boards of trustees are often unaware of the legal procedures required to effect the removal of such items. Many attorneys, even when employed by state or local governing bodies, are not aware of the procedures to determine whether or not a work is obscene under the law. According to U.S. Supreme Court decisions, a work is not obscene until found to be so by a court of law, and only after an adversary hearing to determine the question of obscenity. Until a work is specifically found to be unprotected by the First Amendment, the title remains a legal library acquisition and need not be removed.

In 1971, several attempts to ban publications from libraries involved charges that the works were obscene, and therefore not legal or proper acquisitions for the library. In Groton, Connecticut, in a case involving *Evergreen Review*, the librarian and the board of trustees were threatened with prosecution under a state obscenity statute if they refused to remove the magazine from the library. The board, after several months of resisting efforts to remove the magazine, capitulated in the face of this threat to prosecute them as individuals.

The Groton, Connecticut, case prompted the Intellectual Freedom Committee, with the aid of legal counsel, to study U.S. Supreme Court and federal circuit court decisions concerning procedures whereby materials are determined to be obscene. Four cases in particular were reviewed: Bantam Books, Inc. v. Sullivan (372 U.S. 58, 83 S. Ct. 631, 9 L. Ed.2d

584 [1963]); Marcus v. Search Warrants (367 U.S. 717, 732; 81 S. Ct. 1708, 1716; 7 L. Ed.2d 1127); A Quantity of Copies of Books v. Kansas (378 U.S. 205, 211; 84 S. Ct. 1723, 12 L. Ed.2d 809); and Metzger v. Pearcy (693 F.2d 202 [7 Cir.]).

Using the language of these four decisions as a basis, the Intellectual Freedom Committee developed the "Resolution on Challenged Materials." The statement was submitted to the ALA Council during the 1971 Annual Conference in Dallas, and was adopted as an ALA policy on June 25, 1971.

RESOLUTION ON CHALLENGED MATERIALS
An Interpretation of the "Library Bill of Rights"

WHEREAS, The "Library Bill of Rights" states that no library materials should be proscribed or removed because of partisan or doctrinal disapproval; and

WHEREAS, Constitutionally protected expression is often separated from unprotected expression only by a dim and uncertain line; and

WHEREAS, Any attempt, be it legal or extra-legal, to regulate or suppress material must be closely scrutinized to the end that protected expression is not abridged in the process; and

WHEREAS, The Constitution requires a procedure designed to focus searchingly on the question before speech can be suppressed; and

WHEREAS, The dissemination of a particular work which is alleged to be unprotected should be completely undisturbed until an independent determination has been made by a judicial officer, including an adversary hearing,

THEREFORE, THE PREMISES CONSIDERED, BE IT RESOLVED, That the American Library Association declares as a matter of firm principle that no challenged library material should be removed from any library under any legal or extra-legal pressure, save after an independent determination by a judicial officer in a court of competent jurisdiction and only after an adversary hearing, in accordance with well-established principles of law.

Adopted June 25, 1971, by the ALA Council.

Restricted Access to Library Materials

On January 11, 1971, the City Council of San Jose, California, received a formal request from T. J. Owens, president of the San Jose branch of the National Association for the Advancement of Colored People (NAACP), that the book *Epaminondas and His Auntie* be removed from general circulation in the San Jose libraries. Mr. Owens charged that the book depicts a black child in a manner that makes him look "completely idiotic and stupid."[1]

Subsequent to a discussion of the book with Mr. Owens, Homer L. Fletcher, city librarian, recommended to the city council that *Epaminondas and His Auntie* be retained on open shelf in all the city's libraries and that the option remain for children's librarians to reorder the book should they choose to do so. Mr. Fletcher's recommendation was based on his view that any other action would be inconsistent with the "Library Bill of Rights," which states that "no library materials should be proscribed or removed from libraries because of partisan or doctrinal disapproval" (pt.1, p.11). Despite the recommendation of Mr. Fletcher, the San Jose City Council voted to remove the book from general circulation in city libraries, and to put the book on reserve, thereby necessitating that each individual who wished to use it make a special request to the librarian.

An advisory statement concerning restricted circulation of library materials, drafted in response to the problem in San Jose, was approved by the Intellectual Freedom Committee during the 1971 ALA Annual Conference in Dallas. This statement, in slightly amended form, was submitted to the Council at the 1973 Midwinter Meeting in Washington, D.C., and approved as an ALA policy on February 2, 1973.

1. *San Jose News* March 2, 1971.

RESTRICTED ACCESS TO LIBRARY MATERIALS

An Interpretation of the "Library Bill of Rights"

Restricting access of certain titles and certain classes of library materials is a practice common to many libraries in the United States. Collections of these materials are referred to by a variety of names such as "closed shelf," "locked case," "adults only," or "restricted shelf" collections.

Three reasons generally advanced to justify restricted access are:

1. It provides a refuge for materials that belong in the collection but which may be considered "objectionable" by some library patrons.
2. It provides a means for controlling distribution of materials which alledgedly should not be read by those who are not "prepared" for such materials by experience, education, or age.
3. It provides a means to protect certain materials from theft and mutilation.

Though widely used—and often practical—restricted access to library materials is frequently in opposition to the principles of intellectual freedom. While the limitation differs from direct censorship activities, such as removal of library materials or refusal to purchase certain publications, it nonetheless constitutes censorship, albeit a subtle form. As a form of censorship, restricted access violates the spirit of the "Library Bill of Rights" in the following ways:

1. It violates that portion of Article 2 which states that "no library materials should be proscribed . . . because of partisan or doctrinal disapproval."

   The word "proscribed," as used in Article 2, means

Adopted February 2, 1973, by the ALA Council.

"suppressed." Restricted access achieves *de facto* suppression of certain materials.

Even when a title is listed in the card catalog with a reference to its restricted shelf status, a barrier is placed between the patron and the publication. Because a majority of materials placed in restricted collections deal with controversial, unusual, or "sensitive" subjects, asking a librarian or circulation clerk for them is an embarrassment for patrons desiring the materials. Because restricted collections are often composed of materials which some library patrons consider "objectionable," the potential user is predisposed to thinking of the materials as "objectionable," and is accordingly inhibited from asking for them. Although the barrier between the materials and the patron is psychological, it is nonetheless a tangible limitation on his access to information.

2. It violates Article 5, which states that "the rights of an individual to the use of a library should not be denied or abridged because of his age . . . ."

   Limiting access of certain materials to adults only abridges the use of the library for minors. "Use of the library" includes use of, and access to, library materials. Such restrictions are generally instituted under the assumption that certain materials are "harmful" to minors, or in an effort to avoid controversy with parents who might think so.

   The librarian who would restrict the availability of materials to minors because of actual or suspected parental objection should bear in mind that he is not *in loco parentis* in his position as librarian. The American Library Association holds that it is the parent—and only the parent—who may restrict his children—and only his children—in reading matter. The parent who would rather his child did not read certain materials or certain kinds of materials should so advise the child.*

When restricted access is implemented to protect materials from theft or mutilation, the use of the practice may be legitimate. However, segregation of materials to protect them must be administered with extreme attention to the rationale

---

* See also "Free Access to Libraries for Minors," adopted June 30, 1972, by the ALA Council.

for restricting access. Too often only "controversial" materials are the subject of such segregation, leading to the conclusion that factors other than theft and mutilation were the true considerations. The distinction is extremely difficult to make, both for the librarian and the patron.

Selection policies, carefully developed on the basis of principles of intellectual freedom and the "Library Bill of Rights," should not be vitiated by administrative practices such as restricted access.

Intellectual Freedom Statement

The "Intellectual Freedom Statement" is the most comprehensive of all the ALA policy statements designated "Interpretations of the 'Library Bill of Rights.' " As conceived by the Intellectual Freedom Committee, its purpose was to meet challenges to unrestricted library service foreseen arising in the 1970s. Changes in the American social climate, including evidence of increasing conservatism, and dissatisfaction with certain parts of the 1953 "Freedom to Read" led to the Committee's decision in 1968 to consider preparing of a new statement affirming the freedom to read. (See The Freedom to Read, pt.1, p.10–13.) Like the 1972 revision of "The Freedom to Read," the "Intellectual Freedom Statement" is based on the historic 1953 "Freedom to Read." Unlike "The Freedom to Read," however, it is a position paper applicable exclusively to library service and the library profession.

Articles 4 and 7 of the "Intellectual Freedom Statement" reflect the growing militancy of the ALA. In 1944, when the Association first opposed banning or removing library materials by amending the "Library's Bill of Rights," the ALA Council approved a plan of action to counter violations of the "Library's Bill of Rights." At that time, however, the Intellectual Freedom Committee raised a question, What can the Association do to combat such violations? In answer to its own question, the Committee stated, first, that although having only moral force, the Association should exercise this force; second, that it should publicize every attempt at suppression; and third, that it should compile a record of attempts to obstruct the principle of free inquiry, and should distribute this record to the press.

Since the establishment of its independent, legal-action ally, the Freedom to Read Foundation, the Association has had more than moral force. The Foundation, which endorsed the "Intellectual Freedom Statement" in 1971, has as one of its purposes to challenge in court statutes in force that restrict or make illegal applications of the principles of intellectual freedom to library service. It is also one of the Foundation's purposes to aid with finances and legal counsel any librarian who suffers an injustice because of his stand in defense of the principles of intellectual freedom.

INTELLECTUAL FREEDOM STATEMENT

An Interpretation of the "Library Bill of Rights"

The heritage of free men is ours.

In the Bill of Rights to the United States Constitution, the founders of our nation proclaimed certain fundamental freedoms to be essential to our form of government. Primary among these is the freedom of expression, specifically the right to publish diverse opinions and the right to unrestricted access to those opinions. As citizens committed to the full and free use of all communications media and as professional persons responsible for making the content of those media accessible to all without prejudice, we, the undersigned, wish to assert the public interest in the preservation of freedom of expression.

Through continuing judicial interpretations of the First Amendment to the United States Constitution, full freedom of expression has been guaranteed. Every American who aspires to the success of our experiment in democracy—who has faith in the political and social integrity of free men—must stand firm on those Constitutional guarantees of essential rights. Such Americans can be expected to fulfill the responsibilities implicit in those rights.

We, therefore, affirm these propositions:

1. We will make available to everyone who needs or desires them the widest possible diversity of views and modes of expression, including those which are strange, unorthodox or unpopular.

   Creative thought is, by its nature, new. New ideas are always different and, to some people, distressing and even threatening. The creator of every new idea is likely to be regarded as unconventional—occasionally

Adopted June 25, 1971, by the ALA Council. Endorsed June 18, 1971, by the Board of Trustees, Freedom to Read Foundation.

heretical—until his idea is first examined, then refined, then tested in its political, social or moral applications. The characteristic ability of our governmental system to adapt to necessary change is vastly strengthened by the option of the people to choose freely from among conflicting opinions. To stifle non-conformist ideas at their inception would be to end the democratic process. Only through continuous weighing and selection from among opposing views can free individuals obtain the strength needed for intelligent, constructive decisions and actions. In short, we need to understand not only what we believe, but why we believe as we do.

2. We need not endorse every idea contained in the materials we produce and make available.

We serve the educational process by disseminating the knowledge and wisdom required for the growth of the mind and the expansion of learning. For us to employ our own political, moral, or esthetic views as standards for determining what materials are published or circulated conflicts with the public interest. We cannot foster true education by imposing on others the structure and content of our own opinions. We must preserve and enhance the people's right to a broader range of ideas than those held by any librarian or publisher or church or government. We hold that it is wrong to limit any person to those ideas and that information another believes to be true, good, and proper.

3. We regard as irrelevant to the acceptance and distribution of any creative work the personal history or political affiliations of the author or others responsible for it or its publication.

A work of art must be judged solely on its own merits. Creativity cannot flourish if its appraisal and acceptance by the community is influenced by the political views or private lives of the artists or the creators. A society that allows blacklists to be compiled and used to silence writers and artists cannot exist as a free society.

4. With every available legal means, we will challenge laws or governmental action restricting or prohibiting the publication of certain materials or limiting free access to such materials.

Our society has no place for legislative efforts to coerce the taste of its members, to restrict adults to reading matter deemed suitable only for children, or to inhibit the efforts of creative persons in their attempts to achieve artistic perfection. When we prevent serious artists from dealing with truth as they see it, we stifle creative endeavor at its source. Those who direct and control the intellectual development of our children—parents, teachers, religious leaders, scientists, philosophers, statesmen—must assume the responsibility for preparing young people to cope with life as it is and to face the diversity of experience to which they will be exposed as they mature. This is an affirmative responsibility that cannot be discharged easily, certainly not with the added burden of curtailing one's access to art, literature, and opinion. Tastes differ. Taste, like morality, cannot be controlled by government, for governmental action, devised to suit the demands of one group, thereby limits the freedom of all others.

5. We oppose labeling any work of literature or art, or any persons responsible for its creation, as subversive, dangerous, or otherwise undesirable.

   Labeling attempts to predispose users of the various media of communication, and to ultimately close off a path to knowledge. Labeling rests on the assumption that persons exist who have a special wisdom, and who, therefore, can be permitted to determine what will have good and bad effects on other people. But freedom of expression rests on the premise of ideas vying in the open marketplace for acceptance, change, or rejection by individuals. Free men choose this path.

6. We, as guardians of intellectual freedom, oppose and will resist every encroachment upon that freedom by individuals or groups, private or official.

   It is inevitable in the give-and-take of the democratic process that the political, moral, and esthetic preferences of a person or group will conflict occasionally with those of others. A fundamental premise of our free society is that each citizen is privileged to decide those opinions to which he will adhere or which he will recommend to the members of a privately organized group or association. But no private group may usurp the law and impose its own political or moral concepts upon the general public. Freedom cannot be accorded only to selected groups for it is then transmuted into privilege and unwarranted license.

7. Both as citizens and professionals, we will strive by all legitimate means open to us to be relieved of the threat of personal, economic, and legal reprisals resulting from our support and defense of the principles of intellectual freedom.

Those who refuse to compromise their ideals in support of intellectual freedom have often suffered dismissals from employment, forced resignations, boycotts of products and establishments, and other invidious forms of punishment. We perceive the admirable, often lonely, refusal to succumb to threats of punitive action as the highest form of true professionalism: dedication to the cause of intellectual freedom and the preservation of vital human and civil liberties.

In our various capacities, we will actively resist incursions against the full exercise of our professional responsibility for creating and maintaining an intellectual environment which fosters unrestrained creative endeavor and true freedom of choice and access for all members of the community.

We state these propositions with conviction, not as easy generalizations. We advance a noble claim for the value of ideas, freely expressed, as embodied in books and other kinds of communications. We do this in our belief that a free intellectual climate fosters creative endeavors capable of enormous variety, beauty, and usefulness, and thus worthy of support and preservation. We recognize that application of these propositions may encourage the dissemination of ideas and forms of expression that will be frightening or abhorrent to some. We believe that what people read, view, and hear is a critically important issue. We recognize, too, that ideas can be dangerous. It may be, however, that they are effectually dangerous only when opposing ideas are suppressed. Freedom, in its many facets, is a precarious course. We espouse it heartily.

Part 2
Freedom to Read

The Freedom to Read

"The Freedom to Read," best known of the American Library Association's documents supporting the principles of intellectual freedom as embodied in the "Library Bill of Rights," had its beginnings during the Intellectual Freedom Committee's 1953 Midwinter Meeting in Chicago.[1] At that meeting, Chairman William S. Dix suggested the Committee "discuss the current wave of censorship and attacks on books and libraries"; "help clarify the stand which libraries might take and point to ways in which our own position might be strengthened in the minds of the public." The Committee directed Mr. Dix to consider a small, off-the-record conference with in-depth discussion of the matter.

Mr. Dix's efforts resulted in a conference on the freedom to read, sponsored jointly by the American Library Association and the American Book Publishers Council, held at the Westchester Country Club, Rye, New York, May 2–3, 1953. The object of the meeting was to bring together nationally known figures representing librarians, publishers, and the public interest. Spokesmen for the public interest, viewed as vitally important to the success of the conference, included representatives of business, foundations, law, and education. Luther Evans, former Librarian of Congress and head of the United Nations Educational, Scientific and Cultural Organization, served as chairman of the conference.

In their invitation to potential participants, the joint-sponsors said:

1. For full details of national and international events surrounding for development of "The Freedom to Read," see Everett T. Moore, "Intellectual Freedom," in *Research Librarianship: Essays in Honor of Robert B. Downs*, ed. Jerrold Orne (New York: Bowker, 1971).

Recent months have seen the emergence in our country of a pattern of pressures whose effect must be to limit the range and variety of expression. This pattern has affected in one way or another all the media of communications and indeed the entire area of free inquiry. Books are the last of the communications media to be affected by these pressures toward conformity. They remain preeminently the medium for the free expression of facts, ideas and human experience in all its varieties. Librarians and publishers feel a deep responsibility for doing their part to see that this continues to be so, and they share with thoughtful men in every profession a conviction that freedom of communication is indispensable to a creative culture and a free society.

The objectives of the conference were the following:

1. To define the rights and responsibilities of publishers and librarians in maintaining the freedom of Americans to read what they choose;

2. To assay recent developments tending to restrict this freedom;

3. To consider where lines should be drawn between permissible expression and impermissible expression, and who is to draw the lines; and

4. To ascertain the public interest in this area and, if the group agrees, consider ways of asserting it.

Debate at the conference focused on the specific problem areas of obscenity and pornography and disloyalty and subversive materials. The participants considered a number of questions: What is the function of publishers and librarians in circulating ideas? Should they be responsible guides, or simply caterers to public taste? Do they have a special responsibility to make available nonconforming expression and unpopular views? Do citizens have a right to read everything not expressly prohibited by law? Should a book be judged only by its content, and the political and personal background of the author ignored? Is the role of the public library entirely neutral? Can books be subversive?

The conference resulted in substantial agreement on principles. A Continuations Committee was appointed to draft a statement based on the proceedings and to consider action and research projects designed to publicize and explore further the matters discussed. The Continuations Committee consisted of Arthur A. Houghton, Jr., president of Steuben Glass; Harold D. Lasswell, professor of law and political science at Yale Law School; Bernard Berelson, director of the Behavioral Sciences Division at the Ford Foundation; William S. Dix, librarian at Princeton University; and Dan Lacy, managing director of the American Book Publishers Council.

By the end of May, the Continuations Committee, with the assistance of other individuals, produced a final version of "The Freedom to Read" for the approval of the Westchester Conference participants. On June 18, 1953, the following statement was endorsed by the Board of Directors of the American Book Publishers Council and on June 25, 1953, by the Council of the American Library Association:

> The freedom to read is essential to our democracy. It is under attack. Private groups and public authorities in various parts of the country are working to remove books from sale, to censor textbooks, to label "controversial" books, to distribute lists of "objectionable" books or authors, and to purge libraries. These actions apparently rise from a view that our national tradition of free expression is no longer valid; that censorship and suppression are needed to avoid the subversion of politics and the corruption of morals. We, as citizens devoted to the use of books and as librarians and publishers responsible for disseminating them, wish to assert the public interest in the preservation of the freedom to read.
>
> We are deeply concerned about these attempts at suppression. Most such attempts rest on a denial of the fundamental premise of democracy: that the ordinary citizen, by exercising his critical judgment, will accept the good and reject the bad. The censors, public and private, assume that they should determine what is good and what is bad for their fellow-citizens.
>
> We trust Americans to recognize propaganda, and to reject obscenity. We do not believe they need the help of censors to assist them in this task. We do not believe they are prepared to sacrifice their heritage of a free press in order to be "protected" against what others think may be bad for them. We believe they still favor free enterprise in ideas and expression.
>
> We are aware, of course, that books are not alone in being subjected to efforts at suppression. We are aware that these efforts are related to a larger pattern

5

of pressures being brought against education, the press, films, radio, and television. The problem is not only one of actual censorship. The shadow of fear cast by these pressures leads, we suspect, to an even larger voluntary curtailment of expression by those who seek to avoid controversy.

Such pressure toward conformity is perhaps natural to a time of uneasy change and pervading fear. Especially when so many of our apprehensions are directed against an ideology, the expression of a dissident idea becomes a thing feared in itself, and we tend to move against it as against a hostile deed, with suppression.

And yet suppression is never more dangerous than in such a time of social tension. Freedom has given the United States the elasticity to endure strain. Freedom keeps open the path of novel and creative solutions, and enables change to come by choice. Every silencing of a heresy, every enforcement of an orthodoxy, diminishes the toughness and resilience of our society and leaves it the less able to deal with stress.

Now as always in our history, books are among our greatest instruments of freedom. They are almost the only means for making generally available ideas or manners of expression that can initially command only a small audience. They are the natural medium for the new idea and the untried voice from which come the original contributions to social growth. They are essential to the extended discussion which serious thought requires, and to the accumulation of knowledge and ideas into organized collections.

We believe that free communication is essential to the preservation of a free society and a creative culture. We believe that these pressures towards conformity present the danger of limiting the range and variety of inquiry and expression on which our democracy and our culture depend. We believe that every American community must jealously guard the freedom to publish and to circulate, in order to preserve its own freedom to read. We believe that publishers and librarians have a profound responsibility to give validity to that freedom to read by making it possible for the reader to choose freely from a variety of offerings.

The freedom to read is guaranteed by the Constitution. Those with faith in free men will stand firm on these constitutional guarantees of essential rights and will exercise the responsibilities that accompany these rights.

We therefore affirm these propositions:

1. It is in the public interest for publishers and librarians to make available the widest diversity of views and expressions, including those which are unorthodox or unpopular with the majority.

    Creative thought is by definition new, and what is new is different. The bearer of every new thought is a rebel until his idea is refined and tested. Totalitarian systems attempt to maintain themselves in power by the ruthless suppression of any concept which challenges the established orthodoxy. The power of a democratic system to adapt to change is vastly strengthened by the freedom of its citizens to choose widely from among conflicting opinions offered freely to them. To stifle every nonconformist idea at birth would mark the end of the democratic process. Furthermore, only through the constant activity of weighing and selecting can the democratic mind attain the strength demanded by times like these. We need to know not only what we believe but why we believe it.

2. Publishers and librarians do not need to endorse every idea or presentation contained in the books they make available. It would conflict with the public interest for them to establish their own political, moral, or aesthetic views as the sole standard for determining what books should be published or circulated.

    Publishers and librarians serve the educational process by helping to make available knowledge and ideas required for the growth of the mind and the increase of learning. They do not foster education by imposing as mentors the patterns of their own thought. The people should have the freedom to read and consider a broader range of ideas than those that may be held by any single librarian or publisher or government or church. It is wrong that what one man can read should be confined to what another thinks proper.

3. It is contrary to the public interest for publishers or librarians to determine the acceptability of a book solely on the basis of the personal history or political affiliations of the author.

    A book should be judged as a book. No art or literature can flourish if it is to be measured by the political views or private lives of its creators. No society of free men can flourish which draws up lists of writers to whom it will not listen, whatever they may have to say.

4. The present laws dealing with obscenity should be vigorously enforced. Beyond that, there is no place in our society for extra-legal efforts to coerce the taste of others, to confine adults to the reading matter deemed suitable for adolescents, or to inhibit the efforts of writers to achieve artistic expression.

To some, much of modern literature is shocking. But is not much of life itself shocking? We cut off literature at the source if we prevent serious artists from dealing with the stuff of life. Parents and teachers have a responsibility to prepare the young to meet the diversity of experiences in life to which they will be exposed, as they have a responsibility to help them learn to think critically for themselves. These are affirmative responsibilities, not to be discharged simply by preventing them from reading works for which they are not yet prepared. In these matters taste differs, and taste cannot be legislated; nor can machinery be devised which will suit the demands of one group without limiting the freedom of others. We deplore the catering to the immature, the retarded, or the maladjusted taste. But those concerned with freedom have the responsibility of seeing to it that each individual book or publication, whatever its contents, price or method of distribution, is dealt with in accordance with due process of law.

5. It is not in the public interest to force a reader to accept with any book the prejudgment of a label characterizing the book or author as subversive or dangerous.

The idea of labeling presupposes the existence of individuals or groups with wisdom to determine by authority what is good or bad for the citizen. It presupposes that each individual must be directed in making up his mind about the ideas he examines. But Americans do not need others to do their thinking for them.

6. It is the responsibility of publishers and librarians, as guardians of the people's freedom to read, to contest encroachments upon that freedom by indi-

viduals or groups seeking to impose their own standards or tastes upon the community at large.

It is inevitable in the give and take of the democratic process that the political, the moral, or the aesthetic concepts of an individual or group will occasionally collide with those of another individual or group. In a free society each individual is free to determine for himself what he wishes to read, and each group is free to determine what it will recommend to its freely associated members. But no group has the right to take the law into its own hands, and to impose its own concept of politics or morality upon other members of a democratic society. Freedom is no freedom if it is accorded only to the accepted and the inoffensive.

7. It is the responsibility of publishers and librarians to give full meaning to the freedom to read by providing books that enrich the quality of thought and expression. By the exercise of this affirmative responsibility, bookmen can demonstrate that the answer to a bad book is a good one, the answer to a bad idea is a good one.

The freedom to read is of little consequence when expended on the trivial; it is frustrated when the reader cannot obtain matter fit for his purpose. What is needed is not only the absence of restraint, but the positive provision of opportunity for the people to read the best that has been thought and said. Books are the major channel by which the intellectual inheritance is handed down, and the principal means of its testing and growth. The defense of their freedom and integrity, and the enlargement of their service to society, requires of all bookmen the utmost of their faculties, and deserves of all citizens the fullest of their support.

We state these propositions neither lightly nor as easy generalizations. We here stake out a lofty claim for the value of books. We do so because we believe that they are good, possessed of enormous variety and usefulness, worthy of cherishing and keeping free. We realize that the application of these propositions may mean the dissemination of ideas and manners of expression that are repugnant to many persons. We do not state these propositions in the comfortable belief that what people read is unimportant. We believe

9

rather that what people read is deeply important; that ideas can be dangerous; but that the suppression of ideas is fatal to a democratic society. Freedom itself is a dangerous way of life, but it is ours.

Subsequently, "The Freedom to Read" was endorsed by many other organizations, including the American Booksellers Association, the Book Manufacturers' Institute, and the National Education Association.

For nearly twenty years, "The Freedom to Read" stood as the chief support of the principles enunciated in the "Library Bill of Rights." In the late 1960s, however, several events led to consideration of either a revision of "The Freedom to Read" or a new position paper.

From a deceptively comfortable position in the middle of the 1960s, most librarians looked forward to the 1970s with optimism, hoping for a favorable climate for intellectual freedom. The U.S. Supreme Court extended constitutional support and protection in many areas of human and civil rights. Very encouraging to librarians was the expansion of freedom of expression and other First Amendment rights to allow publications that could not have been found fifteen years earlier. An unfettered climate in which all ideas could be freely exchanged seemed imminent.

But the sense of optimism was soon undercut as increased American involvement in the Vietnam war prompted rancorous divisions among citizens and members of the government. And then came 1968: On April 4, Dr. Martin Luther King was assassinated in Memphis, and the riots provoked in Washington, D.C., led President Johnson to call out troops. By April 14, violence had erupted in twenty-nine states. On June 6, Robert F. Kennedy died in Los Angeles from an assassin's bullet. From August 25 to 29, the Democratic National Convention in Chicago became the scene for violent clashes between the police and National Guard troops on one side and over ten thousand antiwar demonstrators on the other. This period of violent dissent, countered by equally violent reactions, continued into 1970 with the Kent State and Jackson, Mississippi, incidents and battles between Black Panthers and police, and between Weathermen and police.

It became increasingly clear that such incidents of violent dissent and violent reactions, were gradually eroding prospects for the open society many had envisioned. The "permissive" atmosphere collided with demands for law and order. One effect of the collision was that, little by little, the supports in the society at large for intellectual freedom were weakened.

In the form of subpoenas, pressure was brought against news reporters, photographers, and television broadcasting corporations to divulge sources of information and to produce unpublished materials deleted from final reports. Vice President Spiro Agnew gave a series of speeches condemning the news media for biased reporting and calling on citizens to protest such reporting. President Richard Nixon promised to appoint conservatives to the Supreme Court.

Recognizing the increasing conservatism of the nation, and mindful that "The Freedom to Read" might be tied too closely to the McCarthy era, the IFC began, in the fall of 1968, to consider the need for and desirability of a new statement to serve the 1970s. A careful view of the document resulted in the following points:

1. Article 4, urging the vigorous enforcement of "the present laws dealing with obscenity," should be revised or deleted entirely.

2. The basic sentiments expressed in "The Freedom to Read" remain valid and should not be distorted.

3. The document has historical significance.

4. A new statement is needed dealing specifically with the pressures in today's society and those foreseen arising during the next decade.

Believing a new statement should at least be attempted, the IFC contacted the National Book Committee (NBC) and the American Book Publishers Council (ABPC), co-sponsor of "The Freedom to Read," to ask if they were interested in joining the undertaking. Both replied affirmatively. Theodore Waller and Peter Jennison met with the IFC during the 1969 Midwinter Meeting in Washington, D.C., and formed a subcommittee composed of representatives from ABPC, ALA, and NBC, charged with determining content and preparing a draft document.

Meeting during the Atlantic City Conference, June 1969, the subcommittee, composed of Edwin Castagna, Peter Jennison, Judith F. Krug, Dan Lacy, and Theodore Waller, discussed the two major items: (1) Should "The Freedom to Read" be revised, or should a new document be produced? (As did the

IFC, they decided to design a new statement meeting the challenge of the '70s); and (2) What kind of ammunition is needed to meet the challenge of the '70s? The subcommittee also considered such questions as, Can freedom to read be separated from intellectual freedom? Is a broader concept of intellectual freedom, embracing the First Amendment together with other aspects of the Bill of Rights, such as the invasion of privacy, needed? Should all media—not just books—be considered? Should complete intellectual freedom be called for, or, in the end, must one retreat to the principle of the freedom to read?

The subcommittee next met in August of that year, with a membership augmented by the presence of William DeJohn, Freeman Lewis, Harriet Pilpel, and Richard Sullivan. They drafted several statements, and asked Mr. Jennison to assemble them into one cohesive document. Five drafts were subsequently produced, and the IFC, in a mail vote, approved the fifth draft by a ten-to-one vote. At the time of the 1970 Midwinter Meeting, however, a sixth draft had been prepared.

The ABPC Board of Directors received the draft and approved it by acclamation January 28. The sixth draft was resubmitted to the IFC, which approved it by a ten-to-one vote.

Following the 1970 Midwinter Meeting, the staff of the Office for Intellectual Freedom carefully reviewed the sixth draft of the document, tentatively entitled "The Promise of the First Freedom: A Statement of Free Men." The staff could not agree with the IFC's endorsement of this document, and recommended to the IFC that "The Freedom to Read" be revised, as opposed to rewritten, to meet contemporary needs. This decision was based on several factors:

1. The major part of "The Freedom to Read" remained valid.

2. Among those parts that needed change were the specific references to books, for libraries were concerned with all types of materials.

3. Although "The Freedom to Read" had historical significance, subsequent policy statements, as well as actions, of the Association, were in opposition to a few parts, primarily Article 4.

4. The few parts in opposition were believed to be serious matters and should not be permitted to stand.

The revision was undertaken by the Office for Intellectual Freedom and W. Lester Smith of the Association of American Publishers (AAP), successor to the combined ABPC and the American Educational Publishers Institute. The new document differed from the 1953 version on only a few significant points: the earlier call for "vigorous enforcement of present obscenity laws" was omitted, as was the reference to "immature, the retarded, and the maladjusted taste."

The revised "The Freedom to Read" was approved by the ALA Council at the 1972 Midwinter Meeting and by the AAP. It was subsequently endorsed by many other organizations: American Booksellers Association; American Civil Liberties Union; American Federation of Teachers, AFL-CIO; Anti-Defamation League of B'nai B'rith; Association of American University Presses; Bureau of Independent Publishers and Distributors; Children's Book Council; Freedom of Information Center; Freedom to Read Foundation; Magazine Publishers Association; Motion Picture Association of America; National Association of College Stores; National Board of the Young Women's Christian Association of the U.S.A.; National Book Committee; National Council of Negro Women; National Council of Teachers of English; National Library Week Program; P.E.N.—American Center; Periodical and Book Association of America; Sex Information and Education Council of the U.S.; and Women's National Book Association.

THE FREEDOM TO READ

The freedom to read is essential to our democracy. It is continuously under attack. Private groups and public authorities in various parts of the country are working to remove books from sale, to censor textbooks, to label "controversial" books, to distribute lists of "objectionable" books or authors, and to purge libraries. These actions apparently rise from a view that our national tradition of free expression is no longer valid; that censorship and suppression are needed to avoid the subversion of politics and the corruption of morals. We, as citizens devoted to the use of books and as librarians and publishers responsible for disseminating them, wish to assert the public interest in the preservation of the freedom to read.

We are deeply concerned about these attempts at suppression. Most such attempts rest on a denial of the fundamental premise of democracy: that the ordinary citizen, by exercising his critical judgment, will accept the good and reject the bad. The censors, public and private, assume that they should determine what is good and what is bad for their fellow-citizens.

We trust Americans to recognize propaganda, and to reject it. We do not believe they need the help of censors to assist them in this task. We do not believe they are prepared to sacrifice their heritage of a free press in order to be "protected" against what others think may be bad for them. We believe they still favor free enterprise in ideas and expression.

This statement was originally issued in May 1953 by the Westchester Conference of the American Library Association and the American Book Publishers Council, which in 1970 consolidated with the American Educational Publishers Institute to become the Association of American Publishers. Adopted June 25, 1953. Revised January 28, 1972, by the ALA Council.

We are aware, of course, that books are not alone in being subjected to efforts at suppression. We are aware that these efforts are related to a larger pattern of pressures being brought against education, the press, films, radio, and television. The problem is not only one of actual censorship. The shadow of fear cast by these pressures leads, we suspect, to an even larger voluntary curtailment of expression by those who seek to avoid controversy.

Such pressure toward conformity is perhaps natural to a time of uneasy change and pervading fear. Especially when so many of our apprehensions are directed against an ideology, the expression of a dissident idea becomes a thing feared in itself, and we tend to move against it as against a hostile deed, with suppression.

And yet suppression is never more dangerous than in such a time of social tension. Freedom has given the United States the elasticity to endure strain. Freedom keeps open the path of novel and creative solutions, and enables change to come by choice. Every silencing of a heresy, every enforcement of an orthodoxy, diminishes the toughness and resilience of our society and leaves it the less able to deal with stress.

Now as always in our history, books are among our greatest instruments of freedom. They are almost the only means for making generally available ideas or manners of expression that can initially command only a small audience. They are the natural medium for the new idea and the untried voice from which come the original contributions to social growth. They are essential to the extended discussion which serious thought requires, and to the accumulation of knowledge and ideas into organized collections.

We believe that free communication is essential to the preservation of a free society and a creative culture. We believe that these pressures towards conformity present the danger of limiting the range and variety of inquiry and expression on which our democracy and our culture depend. We believe that every American community must jealously guard the freedom to publish and to circulate, in order to preserve its own freedom to read. We believe that publishers and librarians have a profound responsibility to give validity to that freedom to read by making it possible for the readers to choose freely from a variety of offerings.

The freedom to read is guaranteed by the Constitution. Those with faith in free men will stand firm on these constitutional guarantees of essential rights and will exercise the responsibilities that accompany these rights.

We therefore affirm these propositions:

1. It is in the public interest for publishers and librarians to make available the widest diversity of views and expressions, including those which are unorthodox or unpopular with the majority.

   Creative thought is by definition new, and what is new is different. The bearer of every new thought is a rebel until his idea is refined and tested. Totalitarian systems attempt to maintain themselves in power by the ruthless suppression of any concept which challenges the established orthodoxy. The power of a democratic system to adapt to change is vastly strengthened by the freedom of its citizens to choose widely from among conflicting opinions offered freely to them. To stifle every nonconformist idea at birth would mark the end of the democratic process. Furthermore, only through the constant activity of weighing and selecting can the democratic mind attain the strength demanded by times like these. We need to know not only what we believe but why we believe it.

2. Publishers, librarians, and booksellers do not need to endorse every idea or presentation contained in the books they make available. It would conflict with the public interest for them to establish their own political, moral, or aesthetic views as a standard for determining what books should be published or circulated.

   Publishers and librarians serve the educational process by helping to make available knowledge and ideas required for the growth of the mind and the increase of learning. They do not foster education by imposing as mentors the patterns of their own thought. The people should have the freedom to read and consider a broader range of ideas than those that may be held by any single librarian or publisher or government or church. It is wrong that what one man can read should be confined to what another thinks proper.

3. It is contrary to the public interest for publishers or librarians to determine the acceptability of a

book on the basis of the personal history or political affiliations of the author.

A book should be judged as a book. No art or literature can flourish if it is to be measured by the political views or private lives of its creators. No society of free men can flourish which draws up lists of writers to whom it will not listen, whatever they may have to say.

4. There is no place in our society for efforts to coerce the taste of others, to confine adults to the reading matter deemed suitable for adolescents, or to inhibit the efforts of writers to achieve artistic expression.

    To some, much of modern literature is shocking. But is not much of life itself shocking? We cut off literature at the source if we prevent writers from dealing with the stuff of life. Parents and teachers have a responsibility to prepare the young to meet the diversity of experiences in life to which they will be exposed, as they have a responsibility to help them learn to think critically for themselves. These are affirmative responsibilities, not to be discharged simply by preventing them from reading works for which they are not yet prepared. In these matters taste differs, and taste cannot be legislated; nor can machinery be devised which will suit the demands of one group without limiting the freedom of others.

5. It is not in the public interest to force a reader to accept with any book the prejudgment of a label characterizing the book or author as subversive or dangerous.

    The idea of labeling presupposes the existence of individuals or groups with wisdom to determine by authority what is good or bad for the citizen. It presupposes that each individual must be directed in making up his mind about the ideas he examines. But Americans do not need others to do their thinking for them.

6. It is the responsibility of publishers and librarians, as guardians of the people's freedom to read, to contest encroachments upon that freedom by individuals or groups seeking to impose their own standards or tastes upon the community at large.

It is inevitable in the give and take of the democratic process that the political, the moral, or the aesthetic concepts of an individual or group will occasionally collide with those of another individual or group. In a free society each individual is free to determine for himself what he wishes to read, and each group is free to determine what it will recommend to its freely associated members. But no group has the right to take the law into its own hands, and to impose its own concept of politics or morality upon other members of a democratic society. Freedom is no freedom if it is accorded only to the accepted and the inoffensive.

7. It is the responsibility of publishers and librarians to give full meaning to the freedom to read by providing books that enrich the quality and diversity of thought and expression. By the exercise of this affirmative responsibility, bookmen can demonstrate that the answer to a bad book is a good one, the answer to a bad idea is a good one.

The freedom to read is of little consequence when expended on the trivial; it is frustrated when the reader cannot obtain matter fit for his purpose. What is needed is not only the absence of restraint, but the positive provision of opportunity for the people to read the best that has been thought and said. Books are the major channel by which the intellectual inheritance is handed down, and the principal means of its testing and growth. The defense of their freedom and integrity, and the enlargement of their service to society, requires of all bookmen the utmost of their faculties, and deserves of all citizens the fullest of their support.

We state these propositions neither lightly nor as easy generalizations. We here stake out a lofty claim for the value of books. We do so because we believe that they are good, possessed of enormous variety and usefulness, worthy of cherishing and keeping free. We realize that the application of these propositions may mean the dissemination of ideas and manners of expression that are repugnant to many persons. We do not state these propositions in the comfortable belief that what people read is unimportant. We believe rather that what people read is deeply important; that ideas can be dangerous; but that the suppression of ideas is fatal to a democratic society. Freedom itself is a dangerous way of life, but it is ours.

School Library Bill of Rights

During the early 1950s, as the anticommunist reaction of McCarthyism swept across the United States, school librarians and school curriculum planners were affected no less than persons in journalism, entertainment, and government. Schools were coerced to ban works that were alleged to contain "un-American" thinking.

The issue of selecting school library materials was raised during the meeting of the Board of Directors of the American Association of School Librarians (AASL), during the 1953 ALA Annual Conference in Los Angeles. Sue Hefley, chairman of the school libraries discussion group at the second Conference on Intellectual Freedom (held at Whittier College, June 20–21), reported on her group's consensus concerning the need for a policy statement on the matter of selection.

Miss Hefley set forth a number of principles decided upon by the discussion group: liberty is secured and defined in the practice of critical thinking; reading without critical thinking is to abandon freedom of the intellect; a child has the right to read; and if a child is to develop critical thinking, there can be no censorship of subjects or authors in a school library in a democracy. The group determined further that the responsibility for selection should be placed as near as possible to the point of selection, that is, within the school; that advanced provision for considering complaints about materials should be undertaken; and that decisions about complaints should be made by a committee previously chosen from the school community, including parents and non-parents as well as administrative, teaching, and student personnel.

In response to Miss Hefley's report, the board voted "that a committee be appointed to consider the advisability of preparing a statement on book selection in defense of liberty in schools of a democracy, and in considering this problem to make use of the excellent statement prepared at the Conference on Intellectual Freedom. Furthermore, that this committee make recommendations as to what further action AASL should take in this matter."[1]

In preparation for the AASL meeting at the 1954 Annual Conference in Minneapolis, the Committee on Book Selection in Defense of Liberty in Schools of a Democracy submitted a draft for a "School Library Bill of Rights."

At the AASL business meeting on June 24, 1954, the following refined statement was accepted with the understanding that it would be submitted to several educational organizations for evaluation before final adoption:

> In the schools of our democracy, libraries are concerned with the preservation of American freedoms through the development of informed and responsible citizens. To this end the American Association of School Librarians asserts that it is the responsibility of the school library:
>
> To provide materials that will enrich and support the curriculum, taking into consideration the varied interests, abilities, and maturity levels of the children and youth for whom they are selected;
>
> To provide materials for children and youth that will stimulate growth in literary appreciation, in aesthetic values, in ethical standards, and in factual knowledge;
>
> To provide a background of information which will enable children and youth, as citizens, to make wise choices;
>
> To provide objective materials in the areas of opposing viewpoints and controversy, representing all sides of these areas, that as young citizens they may develop the practice of logical, critical thinking and evaluation;
>
> To provide materials which are representative of the many religious, ethnic, and cultural groups and their contributions to our American heritage;
>
> To place principle above personal opinion, reason above prejudice, and judgment above censorship in

1. *School Libraries* 3, no. 1:8 (Oct. 1953).

the selection of materials of the highest quality in order to assure an objective collection appropriate for the users of the library; and

To use democratic practices in the administration of all phases of school libraries as an example for children and young people.

At its business meeting at the 1955 Midwinter Meeting, the AASL officially accepted the "School Library Bill of Rights." This document differed only slightly from the June 1954 draft.

School libraries are concerned with generating understanding of American freedoms and with the preservation of these freedoms through the development of informed and responsible citizens. To this end the American Association of School Librarians reaffirms the "Library Bill of Rights" of the American Library Association and asserts that the responsibility of the school library is:

To provide materials that will enrich and support the curriculum, taking into consideration the varied interests, abilities, and maturity levels of the pupils served;

To provide materials that will stimulate growth in factual knowledge, literary appreciation, aesthetic values, and ethical standards;

To provide a background of information which will enable pupils to make intelligent judgments in their daily life;

To provide materials on opposing sides of controversial issues so that young citizens may develop under guidance the practice of critical reading and thinking;

To provide materials representative of the many religious, ethnic, and cultural groups, and their contributions to our American heritage; and

To place principle above personal opinion and reason above prejudice in the selection of materials of the highest quality in order to ensure a comprehensive collection appropriate for the users of the library.

The action taken by the AASL at its 1955 Midwinter Meeting, however, stated that implementation of the "School Library Bill of Rights" was contingent on the approval of the

ALA Executive Board. In her report to the ALA Council at the 1955 Midwinter meeting, Nancy Jane Day, AASL president, reported that the "School Library Bill of Rights" was being sent to various educational associations and to the ALA Intellectual Freedom Committee for suggestions.

At the 1955 Annual Conference in Philadelphia, Ellenora C. Alexander, a member of the AASL Committee on Book Selection in Schools of a Democracy, reported to the ALA Council that the "School Library Bill of Rights" had been endorsed by the ALA Executive Board and the Intellectual Freedom Committee. Miss Day said that the AASL was "concerned with the pressures brought upon boards of education in the selection of materials, and considered it important to reaffirm the "Library Bill of Rights" of the American Library Association and has developed a bill of rights more specifically applicable to the selection of materials for school libraries." On July 8, 1955, the "School Library Bill of Rights" was adopted by the ALA Council.

In the years following the adoption of the "School Library Bill of Rights," the "Library Bill of Rights" underwent several basic changes. (For full discussion, see Library Bill of Rights, pt.1, p.8–10.) Because of changes in the "Library Bill of Rights," affirmed by the "School Library Bill of Rights" of 1955, as well as changes in the conception of the range of materials to be provided by libraries, the AASL Board of Directors appointed a committee in 1968 to consider revising the 1955 "School Library Bill of Rights."

At the ALA Midwinter Meeting in Washington, D.C., the chairman of the revision committee, Leila Doyle, submitted a tentative draft of the revised "School Library Bill of Rights" to the AASL Board of Directors:

> The professional staff of school media centers is concerned with the development of informed and responsible citizens. To this end the American Association of School Librarians reaffirms the "Library Bill of Rights" of the American Library Association and asserts that the responsibility of the school media center is:
>
> To provide materials that will enrich the student as an individual and support the curriculum, taking into consideration individual needs, and the varied interests, abilities, socioeconomic backgrounds, and maturity levels of the students served;

To provide materials that will stimulate growth in knowledge and develop literary, cultural, and aesthetic appreciations and ethical standards;

To provide materials on all sides of issues, beliefs and ideas so that young citizens may develop the habit of critical thinking, reading, listening, and viewing, thereby enabling them to develop an intellectual integrity in forming judgments;

To provide materials which accurately reflect all religious, social, political, and ethnic groups, and their contribution to our American heritage as well as a knowledge and appreciation of world history and culture; and

To provide comprehensive collections of instructional materials which when selected in compliance with basic selection principles can be defended on the basis of their appropriateness for the users of the media center.

This draft responded to the removal of "of sound factual knowledge" from the "Library Bill of Rights," and included changes in wording reflecting changes in the conception of library service in the schools, service which goes beyond supporting the curriculum.

At the 1969 ALA Annual Conference in Atlantic City, the revised "School Library Bill of Rights" was brought before the AASL Board of Directors. Making only minor corrections, the board voted to accept the revised version of the "School Library Bill of Rights."

SCHOOL LIBRARY BILL OF RIGHTS for School Library Media Center Programs

The American Association of School Librarians reaffirms its belief in the "Library Bill of Rights" of the American Library Association. Media personnel are concerned with generating understanding of American freedoms through the development of informed and responsible citizens. To this end the American Association of School Librarians asserts that the responsibility of the school library media center is:

To provide a comprehensive collection of instructional materials selected in compliance with basic written selection principles, and to provide maximum accessibility to these materials;

To provide materials that will support the curriculum, taking into consideration the individual's needs, and the varied interests, abilities, socioeconomic backgrounds, and maturity levels of the students served;

To provide materials for teachers and students that will encourage growth in knowledge, and that will develop literary, cultural and aesthetic appreciation, and ethical standards;

To provide materials which reflect the ideas and beliefs of religious, social, political, historical, and ethnic groups and their contribution to the American and world heritage and culture, thereby enabling students to develop an intellectual integrity in forming judgments;

To provide a written statement, approved by the local boards of education, of the procedures for meeting the chal-

Approved in 1969 by the American Association of School Librarians Board of Directors.

lenge of censorship of materials in school library media centers; and

To provide qualified professional personnel to serve teachers and students.

Policy on Confidentiality of Library Records

During the spring of 1970, the Milwaukee Public Library was visited by agents of the U.S. Treasury Department requesting permission to examine the circulation records of books and materials on explosives. Initially rebuffed by the assistant librarian, the agents later returned with an opinion from the city attorney's office that circulation records were public records, and that the agents should be allowed access to the files. The library complied. At about the same time, the ALA Office for Intellectual Freedom received reports of similar visits from Treasury Agents at public libraries in Cleveland, Ohio, and Richmond, California. On July 1 of that year, a report was received from Atlanta, Georgia, stating that in the Atlanta area, twenty-seven libraries and branches were visited.

On July 21, the ALA Executive Board issued an emergency advisory statement urging all libraries to make circulation records confidential as a matter of policy. The advisory statement read:

> The American Library Association has been advised that the Internal Revenue Service of the Treasury Department has requested access to the circulation records of public libraries in Atlanta, Georgia, and Milwaukee, Wisconsin, for the purpose of determining the identity of persons reading matter pertaining to the construction of explosive devices. The Association is further advised that such requests were not based on any process, order, or subpoena authorized by federal, civil, criminal, or administrative discovery procedures.
>
> The Executive Board of the ALA believes that the efforts of the federal government to convert library circulation records into "suspect lists" constitute an

unconscionable and unconstitutional invasion of the right of privacy of library patrons and, if permitted to continue, will do irreparable damage to the educational and social value of the libraries of this country. Accordingly, the Executive Board of the American Library Association strongly recommends that the responsible officers in each U.S. library:

1. Formally adopt a policy which specifically recognizes its circulation records to be confidential in nature.

2. Advise all librarians and library employees that such records shall not be made available to any agency of state, federal, or local government except pursuant to such process, order, or subpoena as may be authorized under the authority of, and pursuant to, federal, state, or local law relating to civil, criminal, or administrative discovery procedures or legislative investigatory power.

3. Resist the issuance or enforcement of any such process, order, or subpoena until such time as a proper showing of good cause has been made in a court of competent jurisdiction.

David H. Clift, ALA executive director, and staff members met with Randolph W. Thrower, commissioner of the Internal Revenue Service (IRS), on August 5, 1970, to discuss their mutual concern over the inquiries. Little was agreed upon at the meeting except that "efforts would begin, in a spirit of cooperation, to develop guidelines acceptable to the American Library Association and the Internal Revenue Service." That afternoon, Mr. Clift received a copy of a letter sent to Senator Sam J. Ervin, Jr., chairman of the Senate Subcommittee on Constitutional Rights, by Secretary of the Treasury David M. Kennedy in response to Senator Ervin's earlier expressed concern about the IRS inquiries. Secretary Kennedy's letter stated that the visits had been conducted to "determine the advisability of the use of library records as an investigative technique to assist in quelling bombings. That survey . . . has terminated and will not be repeated." But the door was not being closed on future surveys. The secretary added that "it is our judgment that checking such records in certain limited circumstances is an appropriate investigative technique," and that the Alcohol, Tobacco and

Firearms Division of the Treasury Department has the authority, under federal statute, to conduct limited investigations in specific cases.[1]

ALA indicated its awareness of the Internal Revenue Service's responsibility to enforce the statutes, but noted that the Association's primary concern was not the enforcement itself, but rather, the means by which this enforcement was undertaken regarding libraries. While not intending to hinder effective enforcement of federal statutes, the Association made it clear that circulation records were "not be made available to any agency of state, federal, or local government except pursuant to such process, order, or subpoena as may be authorized under the authority of, and pursuant to, federal, state, or local law relating to civil, criminal, or administrative discovery procedures or legislative investigatory power."

In anticipation of presenting the matter to the ALA Council at the 1971 Midwinter Meeting in Los Angeles, Intellectual Freedom Committee members were polled by telegram in October 1970, concerning a proposed draft of a policy statement. Suggestions for modification of the July statement were made by the IFC and the Executive Board at the latter's 1970 fall meeting. The board suggested that the original introductory paragraph be shortened, that the phrase "and other records identifying the names of library users with specific materials" be added to Article 1, and that Article 3 be clarified.

The "Policy on Confidentiality of Library Records" was formally adopted by the IFC at a special meeting in December 1970. It was submitted to the ALA Council at the 1971 Midwinter Meeting in Los Angeles, and was approved on January 20, 1971. On that date, in his progress report to the Council, IFC Chairman David K. Berninghausen stated:

> When the time comes in any society that government officials seek information as to what people are reading, it must be presumed that they expect to use these records as evidence of dangerous *thinking*. And when a government takes action to control what its citizens are *thinking*, it is a tell-tale sign that all is not well in that society.

1. David M. Kennedy, letter to Sen. Sam J. Ervin, Jr., July 29, 1970 (copy in ALA files).

We recognize that the U.S. Treasury agents probably did not realize that their investigations would be viewed as an invasion of privacy of readers or as an infringement on the freedom of thought guaranteed by the U.S. Constitution and Bill of Rights. But it is such small, beginning steps that lead a nation down the road to tyranny. We are pleased to note that these programs on inquiry have been stopped. We are proud of ALA's prompt action which helped to bring the investigations to an end.[2]

At the 1975 Annual Conference in San Francisco, a new problem of confidentiality was considered by the IFC. Earlier, the Intellectual Freedom Committee of the Washington Library Association had called ALA's attention to the fact that the policy on the confidentiality of library records "identifying the names of library users with specific materials" had been used to justify the release of other kinds of library records on patrons to police officers.

After reviewing this issue, the IFC voted to recommend to Council that the phrase "with specific materials" be deleted from the policy, thus making it applicable to all patron records. This recommendation was accepted by Council at its meeting on July 4, 1975.

2. American Library Association, "Minutes of Council Meetings," mimeographed, p.17.

POLICY ON CONFIDENTIALITY
OF LIBRARY RECORDS

The Council of the American Library Association strongly recommends that the responsible officers of each library in the United States:

1. Formally adopt a policy which specifically recognizes its circulation records and other records identifying the names of library users to be confidential in nature.

2. Advise all librarians and library employees that such records shall not be made available to any agency of state, federal, or local government except pursuant to such process, order, or subpoena as may be authorized under the authority of, and pursuant to, federal, state or local law relating to civil, criminal, or administrative discovery procedures or legislative investigatory power.

3. Resist the issuance or enforcement of any such process, order, or subpoena until such time as a proper showing of good cause has been made in a court of competent jurisdiction.*

---

* Point 3, above, means that upon receipt of such process, order, or subpoena, the library's officers will consult with their legal counsel to determine if such process, order, or subpoena is in proper form and if there is a showing of good cause for its issuance; if the process, order, or subpoena is not in proper form or if good cause has not been shown, they will insist that such defects be cured.

Adopted January 20, 1971, by the ALA Council. Revised July 4, 1975, by the ALA Council.

Resolution on Governmental Intimidation

The issue of the federal government's abuse of authority was brought before the ALA membership at the Association's 1971 Annual Conference in Dallas. At the general membership meeting on June 23, Zoia Horn and Patricia Rom (then librarians at Bucknell University, in Lewisburg, Pennsylvania) introduced a resolution on governmental intimidation. Approved by the membership and two days later amended and approved by the ALA Council, the original ALA statment on governmental intimidation reads as follows:

> WHEREAS, ALA is concerned with the preservation of intellectual freedom; and
>
> WHEREAS, The freedom to think, to communicate, and discuss alternatives are essential elements of intellectual freedom; and
>
> WHEREAS, These freedoms have been threatened by actions of the federal government through the use of informers, electronic surveillance, grand juries, and indictments under the Conspiracy Act of 1968 as demonstrated in the case of the Harrisburg 6, now
>
> THEREFORE BE IT RESOLVED,
>
> 1. That the ALA Membership Meeting at Dallas recognizes the danger to intellectual freedom presented by the use of spying in libraries by government agencies;
>
> 2. That ALA go on record against the use of the grand jury procedure to intimidate anti-Vietnam War activists and people seeking justice for minority communities;
>
> 3. That ALA deplore and go on record against the use of the Conspiracy Act of 1968 as a weapon against the citizens of this country who are being

indicted for such overt acts as meeting, telephoning, discussing alternative methods of bringing about change, and writing letters;

4. That the ALA Membership at Dallas assert the confidentiality of the professional relationships of librarians to the people they serve, that these relationships be respected in the same manner as medical doctors to their patients, lawyers to their clients, priests to the people they serve; and

5. That ALA assert that no librarian would lend himself to a role as informant, whether of voluntarily revealing circulation records or identifying patrons and their reading habits.

In March 1972, the Social Responsibilities Round Table asked the Executive Board to give the Association's moral support and financial aid to a librarian who had been called before a grand jury and had refused to testify. The Social Responsibilities Round Table held that the Dallas "Resolution on Governmental Intimidation" committed the ALA to supporting this librarian. The Executive Board directed the IFC to review the resolution and "develop a statement which would interpret the resolution in terms of guidance for possible action."

At the 1972 Annual Conference in Chicago, the IFC spent a great portion of its scheduled meetings trying to fulfill this charge. The Committee felt that it was unable to develop an interpretive statement because, in the Committee's words, the 1971 statement was "good in intent, but inoperable . . . due to its narrowness of focus." Because the 1971 statement was tied to a specific piece of legislation and a specific incident, the Committee felt the document was difficult to apply. Rather than developing an interpretive statement, the Committee promised to develop a new resolution, expressing similar concerns, for presentation to the ALA Council at the Association's 1973 Midwinter Meeting. The IFC turned its full attention to preparing a new statement at the 1973 Midwinter Meeting. The new document was presented to the Council on February 2, 1973.

The Committee originally moved that the resolution be adopted and substituted in its entirety for the 1971 Dallas statement. However, the Council felt that the new resolution omitted one important concern: an affirmation of the confidential nature of the librarian-patron relationship, covered by Articles 4 and 5 of the Dallas resolution. To ensure that this point was retained as a part of official ALA policy, the Council rescinded all of the Dallas resolution except for Articles 4 and 5. In addition, the Council amended the IFC's resolution, confirming the ALA's support of all those against whom governmental power has been employed. The "Resolution on Governmental Intimidation" was approved by the ALA Council on February 2, 1973.

RESOLUTION ON GOVERNMENTAL INTIMIDATION

WHEREAS, The principle of intellectual freedom protects the rights of free expression of ideas, even those which are in opposition to the policies and actions of government itself; and

WHEREAS, The support of that principle is guaranteed by the First Amendment, thus insuring constitutional protection of individual or collective dissent; and

WHEREAS, Government, at whatever level, national, state, or local, must remain ever vigilant to the protection of that principle; and

WHEREAS, Government, although properly empowered to promulgate, administer, or adjudicate law, has no right to use illicitly its legally constituted powers to coerce, intimidate, or harass the individual or the citizenry from enunciating dissent; and

WHEREAS, The illegitimate uses of legitimate governmental powers have become increasingly a matter of public record, among them being the misuse of the Grand Jury and other investigative procedures, the threat to deny licenses to telecommunications media, the indictment of citizens on charges not relevant to their presumed offenses, and the repressive classification, and hence denial, of documentary material to the very public taxed for its accumulation; and

WHEREAS, These illicit uses not only constitute an abrogation of the right to exercise the principle of freedom of expression but also, and perhaps more dangerously, prefigure a society no longer hospitable to dissent;

Adopted February 2, 1973, by the ALA Council.

NOW THEREFORE BE IT RESOLVED, That the American Library Association, cognizant that in the scales of justice the strength of individual liberty may outweigh the force of power, expresses its unswerving opposition to any use of governmental prerogative which leads to the intimidation of the individual or the citizenry from the exercise of the constitutionally protected right of free expression; and

BE IT FURTHER RESOLVED, That the American Library Association encourages its members to resist such improper uses of governmental power; and

FURTHER, That the American Library Association supports those against whom such governmental power has been employed.

Intellectual Freedom

Intellectual Freedom:
An All-Embracing Concept

When an institution is supported by public funds, taxpayers naturally believe they have the right, if not the obligation, to influence the operations of that institution. Where intellectual freedom is concerned, this belief is especially prevalent, regardless of the kind of library or library activity involved. Too often, however, librarians and others engaged in one particular kind of library or library activity believe their situation is so unique as not to have any relationship to intellectual freedom at all.

The following five articles written by experienced authorities on the philosophy and operation of the most common types of publicly supported libraries—public, school, academic, federal, and state—illustrate that intellectual freedom does indeed affect all types of libraries and library activities. These articles also outline librarians' professional responsibilities with regard to the modifications a particular library environment may impose on the nature and functioning of the all-embracing concept, intellectual freedom.

Public Libraries and Intellectual Freedom

Gerald M. Born

Public libraries differ from most educational institutions in this country. In most educational institutions, the traditional concept of education is based upon the transmission of a preconceived body of knowledge believed necessary to perform a job, live a life, or become a "good" citizen. Education attempts to lead people into this body of information and to impart *in toto* selective and organized knowledge. Education usually provides training within the confines of a particular politics, religion, philosophy, economy, or culture, and is thereby limiting and exclusive. A person, therefore, is considered "well-educated" if he has accepted the tenants, scope, and limitations of the group that has selected the knowledge and is doing the teaching. The public library, on the other hand, seeks to enlighten, to provide truths about the world, to free people from ignorance and error, and to inform and give insight into recorded knowledge. The public library, therefore, imparts no preconceived body of knowledge. Instead, it provides the most up-to-date information available and a multiplicity of differing viewpoints on a wide range of subjects.

Because the public library seeks to enlighten rather than indoctrinate, a basic goal of the institution is the preservation of intellectual freedom. The public library offers the whole spectrum of man's knowledge without moralizing as to its use and without fear of its potential impact on users. It attempts to escape the narrow confines of an imposed way of thinking. There is no starting place; there is no end; there is no "graduation." It offers materials at all levels of development on many subjects of interest and in all forms, to be

Gerald M. Born is the Executive Secretary of the Public Library Association.

studied as superficially or as deeply as a person wishes, needs, or is capable of doing. In this setting, the public librarian is not a teacher, but an expediter of informational exchange.

Schools and universities offer a set curriculum with a degree or certificate when the prescribed body of knowledge is completed. The public library does not. Schools and universities have entrance requirements and fees. The public library does not. It attempts instead to provide a means of developing intelligence and a capacity for independent thinking, for analyzing differing views, and for sifting and relating facts to make value judgments based upon the best information available. The public library assumes an open mind.

Public libraries are firmly rooted in the assumption that, if the world's knowledge is made available to the common man, to a member of the public, he will not only be capable and willing to use that knowledge, but he will also learn from it and thereby become a better man and a better citizen. The founders of the American public library movement believed that knowledge previously the possession of a privileged few should never be so relegated in this country but should be openly and freely available to the common man. Of course, the world was much simpler then, and much of the world's knowledge could be contained in a few thousand volumes. No one could have foreseen the millions of printed, audio, and visual materials that are now turned out yearly, thus compounding the burden of the libraries. Although now libraries must be selective the purpose of the public library remains much the same—to offer man's knowledge to the average citizen who cannot afford, with his own resources, the wide range and great depth of information he must have in a highly organized, scientific, and technological society.

The best way to insure the intellectual freedom of the library's public is to include controversial material that is relevant to the life of the community. If, for instance, abortion is being discussed at the beauty parlor or around the bridge table, material on that subject should be found in the public library. If the "communist threat" and the "yellow peril" are being discussed at the factory, material on every conceivable side of these issues should be found in the library. If "black power" is a familiar phrase, material on blacks and their role in society should be on the shelves. In fact, every issue that touches the community deeply should

5

be amply represented to provide background for rational discussion. Problems of space offer no excuse. Inactive, out-dated material should be discarded so that the public library is a vital force, not the antiseptic, noncontroversial, safe in-stitution that it is all too often.

Based on a philosophy of and belief in creating an en-lightened mind regardless of a person's class or status, public libraries quite naturally become easy targets for censors. If materials and ideas controvert or do not fit the confines of a certain doctrine, or if they threaten the underpinnings of a system, the library is subject to attack. Everything from radical economic views to liberal concepts on sex bring anguished cries. Censorship is not new; every age has had its own censor. A librarian should be comforted by the fact that the works of Greek dramatists, Shakespeare, and James Joyce, the Bible, and even *Peter Rabbit* have been banned at one time or another.

A librarian cannot be unconcerned. He must understand the nature of censorship, the motives of the censors, and what yielding to them means. Public libraries have a profes-sional trust to see that one person or a small group of people do not determine what materials are available to the public at large. The objective of the public library, as outlined by Wheeler and Goldhor, is still valid: "To combat all attempts at censorship, thought control, authoritarianism and class, race or religious prejudice; and to encourage the open mind and respect for individuals regardless of their status."[1]

Before analyzing these sources of censorship external to the library, it should be pointed out that almost every such instance of censorship is motivated by fear. Often confronted by an emotional response to a basically intellectual problem, the librarian must deal with feelings as well as intellectual questions. In many instances, the emotion involved is more pressing than the actual question. A censor is fearful that some library materials may corrupt morals, cause actions jeopardizing an established order, or challenge a religious belief, a philosophical viewpoint, or a deep-seated prejudice.

To deal with censorship problems, it is helpful to analyze the causes of fear. For instance, the man who stole every copy of *Mein Kampf* from a suburban library, thereby becoming a censor, was motivated by the fear that if the book were ac-

---

1. Joseph I. Wheeler and Herbert Goldhor, *Practical Administration of Public Libraries* (New York: Harper and Row, 1962), p.19.

cessible to the public, it would create a situation in the United States like the one that existed in Nazi Germany. His emotional response to the book is understandable as such and can be dealt with only on an emotional plane. Logic and reason would have little effect.

The irate parents discovering that their child has checked out a "dirty" book fear that the child will imitate what he reads and do things of which the parents do not approve. Such a response is quite natural and human; parents are expected to "protect" their offspring. Telling a mother that her good example and upbringing provide the child with the necessary strength to handle the material is much more effective than trying to persuade her of the intellectual reasons for having the book in the collection.

Many censorship problems can be dealt with by calming the patron's fears. Others, however, take careful analysis and a great deal of tact and careful reasoning. These involve the head-on collision of philosophy and modes of thought. Ultimately, the question revolves around a person's right to read what he wants to read for the purpose he wants. In dealing with censorship problems, then, it helps to pinpoint clearly the source of the complaint and to be aware of the broad general groups that account for problems. Broadly classified, these may be characterized as external and internal sources.

The external forces at work in censorship are likely to include:

1. *Parents.* Either singly or in groups, parents may seek to remove materials from a library's collection. Their concern usually centers around materials dealing with sex in an explicit or realistic way and which suggests more license than they wish their children to have. Another kind of materials parents often attack is that cutting across a deep-seated prejudice, such as against interracial marriage.

2. *Religious groups.* Either individual members of a religious affiliation or the group as a whole may attack material. Most often the material raises some moral issue that centers around a sexual deviation from norms the group espouses.

3. *Political groups.* These people attack material favoring political structures different from the one they support. This material includes such a wide range of subject matter that it is difficult to predict what the target will be.

4. *Ethnic groups.* Groups struggling for recognition are apt to want to eliminate anything showing them in a bad light or inaccurately treating their culture.

7

5. *Patriotic groups.* This group protests materials criticizing the government or outlining an alternative to the traditional method.

6. *Emotionally unstable individuals.* Some individuals who are emotionally unstable may focus on any of the above causes as outlets for their frustration. It is important, however, to distinguish whether the underlying cause is a real intellectual confrontation of differing ideas and philosophies or an emotionally upset person who is striking out against the public library as a convenient target.

Censorship pressures may also be brought from inside the institution directly or indirectly. Sources of such pressures include the following:

1. *Trustees or governing bodies.* Since such groups are the policy making bodies, they may build censoring devices into policy. If the board supports a policy of avoiding noncontroversial materials within the library, the librarian is thereby bound to censor such materials in the library. If the board demands the removal of a book because of local pressure, it has established a precedent severely limiting the materials that may be included in a collection. On the other hand, with the support of the board, the librarian can stand up to any would-be censor. Without such support, the library becomes merely a propagandizing agent for the will of the board. When the governing body is negligent of its duty, libraries can now turn to the American Library Association and to the Office for Intellectual Freedom, which assists librarians in trouble.

2. *Library staff.* One of the most difficult kinds of censorship to combat is that imposed by the library's own staff. Besides being catalogers, adult service librarians, children's librarians, and the like, staff members are also parents, churchgoers, and members of political, patriotic, and a great variety of other groups holding particular viewpoints. These may appear threatened, maligned, or ridiculed by material the library owns and materials remain unordered, uncataloged, or uncirculated simply because certain staff members object to them.

3. *Management.* Frequently the attitude of the library management has the effect of censorship. If top administrators shy away from controversial issues, they set the tone for the rest of the staff and very few vanguard materials will be added to the library's collection.

4. *Neglect in selection.* Those who select materials may have limitations because of their background, education, interests, or experience. They may develop a collection along certain lines and totally neglect equally important materials. It is not unusual, for example, to observe a collection built by a selection group with an arty orientation. The library may have a fantastic collection of art and craft books and an impoverished development of science and business titles, thereby excluding a large group of the citizenry. Censorship by neglect of certain subject areas is a common fault in many public libraries.

5. *Restrictive selection policies.* In an age of great social change, when many of the materials being produced do not conform to traditional standards of excellence accepted by the library field, many materials that represent ideas and philosophies not found elsewhere are being left out of collections, thus constituting a form of censorship.

6. *Circulation methods.* Restrictive circulation methods can effect censorship. For example, one public library has a purple daisy to mark those books that should not circulate freely. This simple device assures that only people able to cope with objectionable material have access to it. The problem remains, Who is to determine who is capable of coping with the material? The librarian does not have the training to make this judgment.

7. *Catalogers.* By creating special categories to overcome a "problem" of use, the cataloger can assume a censorship role.

The statement adopted by the ALA Council, "How Libraries Can Resist Censorship," contains the best advice for meeting the censor from outside the library: It recommends a nonrestrictive materials selection policy, a procedure for handling complaints, the maintenance of liaisons with the rest of the community, and a vigorous public relations program on behalf of intellectual freedom (pt.1, p. 36–38).

Internal censorship is a much more delicate matter:

1 and 2. *Trustees or governing bodies and library staff.* The most positive approach is to undertake an educational program, such as a workshop, to assure that trustees, governing personnel, and the staff are aware of the philosophy upon which the public library is built. A basic understanding of the necessity of collecting differing opinions and having free access to them in a democratic society often helps solve some

of the most difficult problems of maintaining intellectual freedom. During the orientation of new staff members, much can be done to show how the public library differs from other educational institutions and how this difference shapes a different kind of collection. As a last resort, the problem can be brought to the American Library Association.

3. *Management.* If it is sensitive to its role in the preservation of intellectual freedom in the community, the board provides a good check and balance to management. The administrator, himself, by continually reevaluating and reexamining his own performance, can find where he stands on important questions. The staff, too, has a role to play in assuming leadership.

4. *Neglect in selection.* The problem of neglect in materials selection can be corrected by turning to outside help. The staff of a state library agency or a system headquarters is usually available to survey and comment on the collection. If such staff is given the task of surveying the collection from an intellectual freedom standpoint, it should be able to give good advice. Outside consultants also specialize in evaluating collections.

5. *Restrictive selection policies.* There should be a constant review and evaluation of selection policies in light of changes taking place in the community. Every social, economic, political, or moral shift creates the need for new materials. The library must keep abreast of the changes through staff involvement, patron surveys, and outside advice in order to make selection policies relevant to community needs.

6 and 7. *Circulation methods and catalogers.* The administrator, with the support of the board, can remove such restrictions by administrative directives.

School Libraries and Intellectual Freedom

Richard L. Darling

School libraries are particularly vulnerable to censorship attempts. Not only is their primary clientele children and youth, but also they are part of a school, an institution to which the general public gives particularly close attention. The schools, especially in recent years, have attracted criticism from virtually all quarters—the political left and right, fundamentalist religious groups, intensely patriotic organizations, and concerned, if sometimes misguided, parents. In such a setting, the school library has had more than its share of critics who profess to protect the forming mind of the young. The chief attacks on school library materials tend to be directed at titles claimed to be un-American, internationalist, or procommunist; to handle sex in too frank and adult a manner; or to present members of minority groups unfavorably. The rise of sex education programs in schools has brought a wave of censorship attempts. Often those opposing sex education attack not only the materials used, but also the instructional program itself.

The problem for the school librarian is complicated because he shares responsibility with the teachers, and both are responsible to higher authorities, the school principal, the school district supervisors and superintendent, and, ultimately, to the board of education. This division of responsi-

Richard L. Darling, Dean of the School of Library Service, Columbia University, was Chairman of the American Library Association Intellectual Freedom Committee from 1971–73. He has served as a consultant on every phase of school library development and was Director of the Department of Educational Media and Technology for the Montgomery County Public Schools in Maryland. The Second Vice-President of the American Library Association from 1970–71 and a past President of the American Association of School Librarians, Mr. Darling was the 1959 recipient of the E. P. Dutton–John McRae Award.

bility probably makes it easier for the would-be censor to attack school library materials with the hope of success.

Because the school library is so vulnerable, school librarians need to plan carefully to protect the integrity of their collection and the integrity of their service to students and teachers. No other type of library so badly needs carefully developed policy for selection of materials. If used in practice, not merely marched out as a means of defense, a good selection policy, approved or adopted by appropriate authority, is a strong bulwark against the censor.

School librarians should seek wide participation of others in preparing their policy statement. The group responsible for its formulation should include students, teachers, and other school personnel, as well as librarians. Certainly, the selection policy writing committee should be appointed by the principal and have his support. When a policy statement has been prepared and accepted within the school, it should be forwarded to the school district central office with the request that board of education approval be sought. In large school districts, a basic selection policy for the entire district may be more practical, especially if an over-burdened school board's approval is to be secured. However, each school should prepare its own elaboration of the basic policy.

The statement itself should be a positive one. Based on the educational goals of the school, it should emphasize the library's contribution to achieving those goals, indicating the types of material the library will acquire and the depth of materials necessary to support each curricular and co-curricular area. It should delineate the library's contribution to instruction and to the growth and development of the young intellect. The policy statement should also indicate the criteria used for evaluating materials and the procedures followed in selecting them.

The selection policy statement should incorporate the "Library Bill of Rights" and the "School Library Bill of Rights" and a statement of the school's affirmation of those basic ALA policies. Not only does this place the school in support of intellectual freedom, but also it provides an opportunity for educating other school personnel in intellectual freedom concepts, helping teachers to see that the integrity of the library is vital to their freedom to teach.

The best policy for selection of materials, duly approved, will not prevent criticism of individual titles. Well-meaning parents and less friendly pressure groups will complain about books or other materials, from time to time. The policy must, therefore, include a procedure for handling complaints. Such complaints should always be written and signed. It is hardly necessary to say that this procedure should be carefully followed no matter how threatening the complainant may appear to be. Books selected for good educational reasons are not likely to be legally banned, so the librarian probably has the law on his side.

Once a school has adopted a selection policy, it should be made available to as wide a public as possible, perhaps through publication in a local newspaper. Failing that, a newspaper should be persuaded to publish a brief article presenting the statement's philosophy and purpose. If possible, librarians should send a copy to the parents of each student and present the policy statement in an assembly program for the students. Even better, the Parent-Teacher Association program chairman should be asked for an opportunity to discuss the statement at a parent meeting. Each teacher should understand it, but it should be presented yearly at the orientation of new teachers. Furthermore, every year a school has new students and new parents who must be informed.

Preparing and using a selection policy statement is the beginning of protecting the student's right of access to library materials. All materials should be classified and cataloged and made available to the students. Nothing selected under a positive selection policy need be restricted in any way. Maintaining a restricted collection truly defeats the educational purpose of a school library, since such a collection inhibits, rather than promotes, education. Some titles will be selected for teachers, but they also should be available to students, at least to the extent that such availability does not prevent teachers from using them. Protecting the intellectual freedom of students by maintaining the school library collection's integrity is a continuing process. The school librarian should make this protection the foundation of the library program.

Academic Libraries and Intellectual Freedom

Since the function of the academic library is to support the teaching and research programs of the college or university of which it forms a part, the degree to which the library enjoys intellectual freedom will be largely determined by the commitment of the parent institution to academic freedom. If the institution is firmly committed to freedom of inquiry in all areas of knowledge, and this commitment has been made a formal policy by the governing body, the library is unlikely to come under attack from would-be censors, and should be able to defend itself successfully if an attack does come. The library, of course, accepts an equally strong obligation to be absolutely certain that neither its formal policies nor the conscious or unconscious biases of its staff violate the intellectual freedom of its constituency. Unhappily, there appears to be full reason to believe that in the academic library, as in all others, the greatest dangers to intellectual freedom are more internal than external.

If the parent institution is not wholly committed to academic freedom, the library should still attempt to practice intellectual freedom principles to the extent that it can. The constituency of an academic library is the student body, faculty, and staff of the parent institution. While most academic libraries provide some service beyond the campus, such service, unless mandated by the charter of a public institution or agreed to by contract, is always a courtesy, not a right, and intellectual freedom is not violated if off-campus

Paul B. Cors is Head of Technical Processes at the Wyoming State University Library in Laramie. He is a member of the American Library Association Intellectual Freedom Committee and has served as a member and Chairman of the Wyoming Library Association Intellectual Freedom Committee.

patrons are not given equal treatment with the library's prime constituency.

It is as important for the academic library, as for any other type, to have for collection development a written policy incorporating the principles of the "Library Bill of Rights." This policy should be drafted by the staff, in cooperation with the faculty library committee if such a group exists, and ratified by the appropriate administrative body of the institution. One common problem can be prevented if the policy states clearly to what extent the library will acquire material of general interest, including recreational reading, for student use. Copies of the policy should be freely available to students and faculty.

It is also important to have a procedure established, and made known to all library staff, for handling complaints about the presence—or absence—of specific titles or subject areas. The standard complaint forms are not altogether applicable to academic libraries without modification. In any case, they are oriented toward the person who wants material removed, not the person who wants material added, and experience suggests that students' complaints are usually of the latter type.

The library's cataloging/processing manual should specify that the organization of a collection must not be used as a tool of censorship. If the collection is basically open-stack, definitions of material to be housed in restricted access areas must be carefully drawn. Classifications and subject headings should accurately reflect content (which may mean that decisions to use Library of Congress headings as they stand will have to be questioned), and all material in the collection should be listed in the public records of the library.

It is in the area of services, not collection development, that academic libraries are more likely to fall short in their devotion to intellectual freedom. In part, this is because of conditions which the library cannot alter: the academic community is a socially stratified community, and this stratification will affect the library. Nevertheless, one of the basic principles of the "Library Bill of Rights" is equality of access, and the library should strive to follow that principle. Therefore, it is necessary that certain traditional policies followed by many—if not most—academic libraries be reexamined. It is of little merit to develop an excellent collection and then to place insurmountable obstacles in the path of those who wish to use that collection.

Circulation policies should be the same for all patrons and should aim at providing adequate time for the use of material without allowing anyone to monopolize an item at the expense of others. Restrictions on the circulation of material such as reference books or rare books are not inherently in violation of intellectual freedom, provided that they apply equally to all. Reference staffs should respond to all requests for assistance with equal diligence, making no distinction based on the "importance" of the patron.

A most difficult question is interlibrary loan. The present "Interlibrary Loan Code," which denies this service to undergraduates, is incompatible with the "Library Bill of Rights." The rationale for this limitation is not altogether indefensible because faculty and graduate research may indeed require access to a wider range of materials than undergraduates normally need, or any one library can supply. However, an attempt to revise the code to remove the conflict and still protect interlibrary loan personnel from inundation by frivolous requests is urgently recommended.

A similar problem is limited access to stacks, though again the reasons for the practice have some validity. Still, policies which provide some users more access to the collection than others enjoy do not conform to the "Library Bill of Rights." Exit checks, disagreeable to all but apparently necessary, should exempt nobody.

Any other specialized services which the library provides should be offered equally to everybody in its constituency. Any fees charged for such services (for example, photocopying) should be uniformly assessed.

The internal administrative procedures of the library, including personnel policies, should foster a spirit of intellectual freedom among all staff members. Whether this is best done informally or through a structured program of in-service training will depend upon the size and character of the staff. Finally, the more clearly the administration exemplifies its own devotion to the cause of intellectual freedom, the more certain it will be that devotion to this cause becomes the foundation for every part of the library program.

Federal Libraries and Intellectual Freedom

Bernadine E. Hoduski

The federal library community is composed of a variety of libraries comparable in type to those in the library community as a whole. Federal libraries range from the one-of-a-kind Library of Congress to small school libraries on Indian reservations and to specialized libraries serving executive agencies.

Federal libraries have censorship problems just like other libraries, but these are seldom brought to the attention of the library profession or the public. The records of the Federal Library Committee do not indicate that any federal library has accepted the "Library Bill of Rights." Many federal librarians feel that there is no problem with censorship in government libraries. Others do not agree. Most of them do agree that positive steps should be taken to help prevent possible censorship situations.

Even though federal libraries differ in many respects, they do have some things in common: (1) They must function according to a number of federal laws and regulations. (2) Their mission is usually dictated by the agency to which they belong. (3) Since they are supported by federal taxes they are answerable, directly or indirectly, to all U.S. citizens.

Federal libraries can prevent many problems, including censorship ones, by following some simple procedures:

1. With the assistance of the agency's lawyer, it should be determined which laws and regulations govern the agency and the library because regulations differ from one agency to the next.

2. An order describing the purpose, functions, and policies

Bernadine E. Hoduski is Librarian of the Environmental Protection Agency in Kansas City, Missouri, and was the founder of the Government Documents Round Table of the American Library Association.

17

of the library should be written, thus officially establishing and protecting the existence of the library. This order should be signed and distributed by the administrator of the agency.

3. Every opportunity should be taken to educate the agency administrator, the staff, and the public as to the policies of the library.

4. The other federal libraries, especially those in the specific agency, should be cooperated with and notes on book selection, circulation policies, and the like compared. Such notes can be used as examples in educating the staff.

5. It should be determined whether the Freedom of Information Act affects the library. Some federal libraries serve as the agency's public reading room in order to fulfill the requirements of the law which states that the public must have reasonable access to documents issued by an agency. If the library is the official repository for agency documents, these have to be made accessible to the public. If the library keeps classified and unclassified documents, some provision will have to be made to keep these separate. Again, the agency's lawyer should be checked with.

6. If possible, a library committee representing all elements of the agency should be set up so that materials selection, circulation policies, and the like will be fair to all. In turn, the library committee can help in educating the rest of the agency and in supporting the library policies.

7. A written circulation policy should be maintained, not favoring one department or group in an agency over another. If the library circulates material to the public, it should be done for everyone, not just for a select few. It may be decided to loan just through another library rather than to individuals. If so, this decision should be publicized. Some agencies, because of regulations, do not allow those outside the agency to use their library.

8. A written materials selection policy should also be maintained. Even though the subject area is often decided by the mission of the agency, the diversity of views in that subject area must be guarded. An obvious example of censorship would be refusal to buy publications critical of an agency.

Because federal libraries are important information links in the decision-making process of the U.S. government, they must be protected from censorship.

State Library Agencies and Intellectual Freedom

Joseph J. Anderson

An important goal of any state library agency is to provide dynamic leadership in developing and maintaining an environment in which the values for which libraries stand can flourish to the benefit of all citizens. In the area of intellectual freedom, the state library agency must set the practical example—through policies and services consistent with the "Library Bill of Rights"—not only for all those within the library but also for all other types of libraries in the state.

The library has always figured prominently in the educational process, whether for early childhood or for advanced age. In today's highly complex and technologically oriented society, with its emphasis on the process of information transfer, the state library agency is obligated to actively foster free exchange of total information and knowledge.

State libraries' collections should reflect a materials selection policy allowing access to controversial, scarce, and esoteric titles from at least one of the library's service locations, whether for direct circulation, interlibrary loan, or photoduplication. Appropriately, the state library acts as the backup resource collection for the state at large, in most cases, and most certainly for resources pertinent to maintaining intellectual freedom.

The public card catalog and other location tools used to organize the collection should employ popular expressions in current usage to insure that access to information is not waylaid by bias. By following the principles of the ALA "Statement on Labeling," which opposes labeling as a form of predisposing readers against specific materials, such bias can be largely eliminated.

Every state library is involved in continuing education programs for librarianship including training programs and

Joseph J. Anderson is the Nevada State Librarian and a member of the American Library Association Intellectual Freedom Committee.

other forms of education for those concerned with library development and management within the state. The concept of intellectual freedom should naturally rate priority in such overall education programs.

State libraries are generally in a position to respond directly to requests for assistance from local libraries, boards, or other citizen groups in matters pertinent to intellectual freedom. State library agency staff can be expected to include persons of sufficient maturity and experience to provide the necessary leadership, direction, and information.

Another major contribution the state library can make on behalf of intellectual freedom is in the area of government, through the library's access to the persons and machinery responsible for decisions and policies. It is important to remember that a state library working across jurisdictional lines can be effective statewide and thus can assist local agencies, as well, by providing access to current information on state government.

Keeping local libraries—and those individuals concerned with their operation and service—informed of all matters pertaining to intellectual freedom, including proposed action before legislatures, attorney generals' opinions, cases at law, and opinions of state supreme courts, is an important function of the state library agency. Such information from the federal and state level can be and is included in the state library for the use of local community leaders.

A working relationship among the state library agency, the state library association, and state or other advisory or regulatory library commissions and councils, together with local boards of library trustees, will go a long way toward maintaining the necessary climate for intellectual freedom. This partnership should provide appropriate advocacy for the concerns of intellectual freedom. Broadly based geographically and politically, such a coalition is free of vested interest, ax grinding, and other stumbling blocks to progress. The state library's role in this respect is to provide information for discussion, to maintain public and political contacts, and to undertake affirmative lobbying efforts.

The positive effects of fighting for a position often outweigh restrictive attempts to curtail intellectual freedom. It is incumbent upon the library leadership of a state to insure that all the values of free access in library and information services operate to benefit the quality of life for all its citizens.

Before the Censor Comes: Essential Preparations

Before the Censor Comes: Essential Preparations

Many challenges to the principles of intellectual freedom go unchecked or are mishandled simply because preparations for an effective response have not been made. An arsenal of defenses must be available at the moment the librarian is confronted by the would-be censor. And if these preparations are to be ready at a moment's notice, they must be in writing and a part of the library's procedures manual.

Why is written policy stressed? First, it encourages stability and continuity in the library's operations. Library staff members may come and go but the procedures manual, kept up-to-date, of course, will help assure smooth transitions when organization or staff changes occur. Second, ambiguity and confusion are far less likely to result if a library's procedures are set down in writing.

Additional and convincing reasons for maintaining written procedures can be outlined:

1. They show everyone that the library is running a businesslike operation.

2. They inform everyone about the library's intent, goals, and aspirations and circumvent ambiguity, confusion, and trouble.

3. They give credence to library actions; people respect what is in writing even though they may not agree with every jot and tittle in the library's procedures manual.

4. They are impersonal; they make whimsical administration difficult.

5. They give the public a means to evaluate library performance; publicly pronounced policy statements prove that the library is willing to be held accountable for its decisions.

6. They contribute to the library's efficiency; many routine decisions can be incorporated into written procedures.

7. They help disarm crackpot critics; the accusations of local cranks seldom prevail when the library's operations are based on clearcut and timely written procedures that reflect thorough research, sound judgment, and careful planning.

If such written procedures are later adopted by the library's governing body, so much the better. But regardless of whether or not the governing body adopts them as policy, three procedures, at least, are vital for the good of the library and the defense of intellectual freedom.

In the following sections the three most essential preparations—developing a materials selection program, a procedure for handling complaints, and a public relations program—are described in depth and practical guidelines are provided. Such preparations are important on a day-to-day basis. If they also have the endorsement of the library's governing body, they provide an even firmer foundation for supporting intellectual freedom in the case of a censorship dispute.

Development of a
Materials Selection Program

The primary purpose of a materials selection program is to promote the development of a collection based on institutional goals and user needs. A secondary purpose is service in defending the principles of intellectual freedom.

The basis of a sound selection program is a materials selection statement. Although a majority of professional librarians believe a materials selection statement is desirable, in too many instances the belief does not become reality. Many reasons for not writing such a statement are given, but often two unmentioned reasons are the most important: lack of knowledge about how to prepare one, and lack of confidence in one's abilities to do so. Regardless of past failures and existing difficulties, however, there is an absolute need for the firm foundation that a selection statement provides.

In virtually every case, it will be the librarian's task to prepare the materials selection statement. Although approval or official adoption of the statement rests with the institution's legally responsible governing body, it is the librarian who has the expertise and practical knowledge of the day-to-day activities of the library.

A materials selection statement must relate to concrete practices. It should, in effect, provide guidelines for strengthening and adding to the library's collection. Furthermore, if the statement is to fulfill its secondary purpose, that of defending intellectual freedom, it must be a viable, working document which relates to the library's day-to-day operations. In the case of very large libraries or even medium-sized institutions with highly sophisticated holdings, the librarian may prefer to separate the policy statement from procedural considerations. Thus, the materials selection statement would reflect institutional policies, while a separate procedures manual would deal with the day-to-day applications of those policies.

A strong collection and intellectual freedom go hand in hand. It is less likely that problems will remain unresolved if the collection reflects the logical, coherent, and explicit statement from which it grows. In developing a materials selection statement, four basic factors must be considered: (1) service policy, (2) environmental characteristics, (3) collection specifications, and (4) current selection needs.

SERVICE POLICY

A service policy will provide practical operational guidelines to govern future collection development in accordance with the needs of the library's users and the goals of the library. In order to establish a service policy, it is necessary to determine what groups the library is striving to serve and what purposes it is attempting to achieve. To do so will entail a study of user-group characteristics and institutional objectives.

I. User groups. A materials selection statement must reflect the needs of the people the library will serve in trying to fulfill its objectives. To establish guidelines for collection development and related library activities, it is necessary to gather detailed information on various user groups.

A questionnaire to establish basic data could be prepared and completed by each staff member working with the public. Or, such information could be compiled on the basis of institutional statistics and records. After the library staff has been surveyed, users can be given questionnaires on their purposes in using the library, their library activities, and the like. It should be noted that certain sections of the prepared form can be used to determine the desired state of affairs as well.

A. Population characteristics
   1. Age
   2. Education

3. Employment level
4. Etc.

B. Size of each user group
C. Primary purpose of each group in using the library
D. Kinds of material used in accomplishing these purposes
E. Kinds of activities engaged in during the accomplishment of these purposes

II. Institutional objectives. The materials selection statement should define the library's goals and reason for existing. There are at least two sources from which institutional goals can be determined.

A. Statements of objectives are ideally available in a public document designed to inform all concerned persons.
   1. General need(s) the library is designated to fulfill
   2. Activities or standards most valued
   3. Distinction in some field of endeavor

   Public documents and records, in lieu of a statement of objectives, may outline the institution's objectives and supplement statements of objectives.
   1. Annual reports of the institution
   2. Charter of the institution
   3. Published history of the institution
   4. Records of the governing body
   5. Budget (Because preparation of a budget usually demands a resolution of difficult questions of priorities in order to allocate scarce resources, this item should not be overlooked.)

ENVIRONMENTAL CHARACTERISTICS

The librarian should determine all aspects of the environment surrounding the institution that could possibly influence the development of the library collection and the library's related activities. A few such environmental factors and their implications are the following:

ENVIRONMENTAL FACTORS	PROVISIONS AFFECTED
Relative geographical isolation	Materials related to the cultural/recreational needs of users
Economic structure	Materials related to specific educational needs
Presence/absence of library resources external to the institution	Degree of self-sufficiency or completeness of materials
Presence/absence of postsecondary learning institutions	Scholarly/technical works
Relationship to local industries	Technical reports and business materials
Relationship to local professional/cultural groups	Specialized subcollections

COLLECTION SPECIFICATIONS

Specifications are to be established for each subject area or area of concern. (The data gathered to determine service policy and environmental characteristics will show, in large measure, what the library requires.) For this section of the selection statement, each subject area should be carefully reviewed in order to determine the types of materials to be acquired in each and the depth in which materials are to be sought. Such a review is especially important in smaller libraries where funds are severely limited and the needs of the users potentially great.

If possible, the following data should be collected for each area:

> number of library materials currently held
> total number of relevant materials available
> percent of total materials held
> distribution of current holdings by publication date

In addition, holdings should be rated by subject area in terms of specific user purposes:

recreation

self-help

continuing education

business

Finally, a desired acquisition level should be specified for each area.

The section of the selection statement dealing with collection specifications will no doubt be the largest and most detailed of all. It will specify the criteria to be used in selecting and reevaluating materials in terms of (1) users' age groups; (2) users' special needs by virtue of occupation, cultural interest, etc.; and (3) types of materials (books, periodicals, newspapers, government publications, maps, records, films, etc.). This section will also specify policies to be used in handling such matters as gifts and special bequests.

CURRENT SELECTION NEEDS

Current selection needs can be determined by the difference between the present collection and the collection specifications. In deciding what is currently needed, the desired state of affairs that may have been detailed under service policy should also be consulted. Once current needs are determined, other considerations come into play. Most prominent among these is the library's budget. Regardless of the amount of money available, the selection statement should indicate in as clear a manner as possible which materials are to be bought and which are not.

After consideration of the above four factors: service policy, environmental characteristics, collection specifications, and current collection needs, the next step is preparing a final draft of the selection statement for the governing body of the library. This draft should contain an affirmation of the "Library Bill of Rights" (or if appropriate, the "School Library Bill of Rights") and "The Freedom to Read" as basic documents governing all library policies. The statement should also include the ALA "Policy on Confidentiality of Library Records," which states that circulation records and other records identifying the names of library users should be considered confidential in nature.

The table of contents of the final draft of the materials selection statement might look like this:

I. General principles of selection
   A. "Library Bill of Rights," "The Freedom to Read," and "Policy on Confidentiality of Library Records"
   B. Institutional objectives
   C. Collection objectives
   D. Responsibility for selection
   E. Policies of selection
      1. Selection for user group A
      2. Selection for user group B
      3. Etc.

II. Special principles of selection
   A. User groups
   B. Form and nature of material
      1. Fiction
      2. Periodicals
      3. Audio-visuals
      4. Etc.
   C. Subject of material

It hardly needs to be said that preparation of a complete statement requires work—lots of it. And the work must be done before the censorship problem arises. Unfortunately, there are no shortcuts. It is impossible to borrow a statement based on another institution's goals and needs. Above all, the statement must be a working document, a handbook for daily activities reflecting the needs of those who are to use it.

Procedures for
Handling Complaints

All librarians must be aware that at some time there will be complaints about library service—and sometimes these complaints will center around a particular book, magazine, or other item which the library distributes. What should one do when a complaint of this kind is made? As in handling any type of complaint about library operations, a courteous and calm approach is essential. Above all, the complainant must know that his objections will be given serious consideration and that his interest in the library is welcome. If the complainant comes by in person or telephones, he should be listened to courteously and invited to file his complaint in writing. If the complaint comes by letter, it should be acknowledged promptly. In either case, he should be offered a prepared questionnaire so that he may submit a formal complaint. In addition, the necessity for having such a formal complaint should be explained.

Having a prepared form is not just an additional piece of record keeping. There are a number of advantages in having a complaint procedure available. First, knowing that a response is ready and that there is a procedure to be followed, the librarian will be relieved of much of the initial panic which inevitably strikes when confronted by an outspoken and, perhaps, irate library patron. Also important, the complaint form asks the complainant to state his objections in logical, unemotional terms, thereby allowing the librarian to evaluate the merits of his objections. In addition, the form benefits the complainant. When a citizen with a complaint is asked to follow an established procedure for lodging his complaint he will feel assured that he is being properly heard and that his objections will be considered.

The accompanying sample complaint form (see figure 1), entitled "Request for Reconsideration of Library Materials,"

Part 4

REQUEST FOR RECONSIDERATION OF LIBRARY MATERIALS

Title_____ ☐Book ☐Periodical ☐Other _____

Author_____

Publisher_____

Request initiated by_____

Address_____

City_____ State_____ Zip_____ Telephone_____

Do you represent:

☐Yourself

☐An organization (name)_____

☐Other group (name) _____

1. To what in the work do you object? (Please be specific. Cite pages.)
_____

2. Did you read the entire work?_____ What parts?_____
_____

3. What do you feel might be the result of reading this work?_____
_____

4. For what age group would you recommend this work?_____
_____

5. What do you believe is the theme of this work?_____
_____

6. Are you aware of judgments of this work by literary critics? _____
_____

7. What would you like your library/school to do about this work?
   ☐Do not assign/lend it to my child.
   ☐Return it to the staff selection committee/department for re-
      evaluation.
   ☐Other. Explain: _____
_____

8. In its place, what work would you recommend that would convey
   as valuable a picture and perspective of the subject treated?

_____

Signature _____

Date _____

Fig. 1. Example of a request for reconsideration form

was adapted by the Office for Intellectual Freedom from several forms, including one developed by the National Council of Teachers of English. Librarians should feel free to reproduce and use it.

The questions asked go beyond simply formalizing the complaint. The first section requests the complainant to identify himself and to reveal the size of his backing. Such facts are important: Is he acting alone or does he represent a local church, citizens' group, or political organization? Questions 1 and 2 inquire about the complainant's explicit objections and his familiarity with the title being challenged. Questions 3 and 4, in addition, request that he evaluate the effect of the work, particularly for groups other than the one he has immediately in mind. Question 5 asks the complainant to state what he feels the theme of the work is. Question 6 inquires about his awareness of the opinions of literary critics. Finally, the last two questions ask what alternative action he would recommend.

As soon as the complaint has been filed, the objections should be reviewed. The review should consist of specific steps, although the number will vary somewhat according to the individual library involved. Simultaneous with the review, the governing body (that is, board of trustees, school board, etc.) should be routinely notified that a formal complaint has been made.

First, the person or committee that selected the item, or an ad hoc committee, should evaluate the original reasons for the purchase. The objections should be considered both in terms of the library's materials selection statement and the opinions of the various reviewing sources used in materials selection. If the materials selection statement is sufficiently detailed to function as a guide for selection decisions, it should not be difficult to make a logical, strong response to the objections.

Second, the objections and the response should be forwarded to the librarian who has final responsibility for ordering materials. He, in turn, should review the response and add his own comments or return the response to the individual or committee for further clarification. At this point, then, either the order librarian or the selection committee can make a written response to the complainant. If the complainant is not satisfied, then the head administrator of the library (the person to whom the governing body has given authority) can serve as the person to whom an initial appeal is made. He should contact the complainant, explaining the decision of the library, and advise the complainant that further discussions are welcome.

If the complainant still feels that his objections have been dealt with inadequately, he can make a final appeal (within the structure of the library) to the governing body of the institution. This body will in turn decide upon an appropriate course of action—for example, a public hearing. It must be emphasized, however, that requests for action from the governing body should not be routine; such requests are best avoided by an adequate first response to the complainant.

Public Relations and the Library

Marion L. Simmons

Public relations, some say, is ninety percent performance and ten percent interpretation. This remark should give a good idea of the amount of effort required to achieve results in the image projected by the institution. In other words, public relations is doing a good job and telling people about it. But what is said is considerably less important than what is done.

Public relations is not a project designed to meet a specific situation like a censorship problem. It is an ongoing and continuing part of the management function of the library. Policies designed to meet established goals and considered in terms of their effect upon the people served form the basis for the public relations program. If the library is large enough to support a public relations officer, that person should meet with the group that recommends policies for the institution.

The first responsibility of the policy making group is to know the community served, whether it is a university or a small college campus and its surrounding community, a high school and the area from which it draws students, a great metropolis, or a wide geographical area. There must be enough research and enough listening to learn the needs of the various publics served. Circles of interest, organizations and their key people, opinion leaders, political figures—all must be identified. This information will also be invaluable later when it is time to interpret the policies and the library's program.

The listening may be done on a person-to-person basis in

Marion L. Simmons has served as Chief of the Public Relations Office of the New York Public Library and is a public relations consultant for libraries.

15

the library, in the faculty dining room, and at meetings of community groups which staff should be encouraged to join. Formal research and survey methods require special skills and are costly. They should be undertaken only with the assistance of professional researchers who may be found within the library's publics. Librarians, as information specialists, can gather much data by careful reading and clipping of local papers and from a variety of reports and directories.

Based on the knowledge gleaned through listening and research, a program of service is designed to implement the policies. The listening process continues as a part of evaluating results in light of long-range goals. But that is ahead of the story.

There should be an effective organization of the public relations function within the library structure. Budgetary support is essential to provide materials and staff, including clerical assistance. There should be continuity of aims and operations. A public relations program cannot be limited to an annual report and celebration of National Library Week. Responsibility for the program must be allocated to one person who coordinates efforts and resources. This person is responsible for planning and programming for both limited and long-range objectives.

No matter where the responsibility for the public relations function lies, at some time each employee is "the library" to someone. The clerk at the desk, the telephone operator, and the reference assistant will sooner or later be interpreting library policy to their own circle of friends, if not to library users. Public relations is everybody's job. A prime responsibility, therefore, is to realize that the staff is one of the most important publics and should be well-informed on policies and goals.

Only with all of this preparation through goals, policies, and services which implement policies, is the library ready for the ten percent which is interpretation. Great care should be taken in the selection and use of public relations techniques for communicating with users, community agencies, opinion leaders, and the general public. The choice will be guided by available resources in budget, staff, and facilities.

Since whatever resources exist never seem to be adequate, the library needs to seek all the help it can find to get the job done. Friends of the Library groups are a natural focus for communicating library information in a widening circle. Providing programs of films, speakers, and story tellers for local groups means reaching an already established audience with known interests. Volunteers may require time consuming training to be useful to the library, but such training results in a new group of well-informed "natural allies."

Certain individuals are well worth the effort of developing them into "natural allies" through special techniques. Just as the university librarian may notify a faculty member of new acquisitions in his field, interest profiles on the president, the chancellor, or the controller could be kept and appropriate material sent them to prove the library's usefulness. The school librarian can use the same technique. The public librarian might send books or copies of articles to the mayor, the budget director, the councilman, the county legislator, or the heads of other city departments with a note suggesting that they or members of their staffs might find the attached information of value. A complaint from a reader, in fact, provides an opportunity to make a new friend and potential active supporter of the library and the patron's response may either clarify a misunderstanding or elicit a new idea on how to provide better service.

Apart from reaching groups and individuals, mass media are the obvious way of keeping people aware of the library. Regularly submitted news stories are vital to any library's community relations. Their effects, like those of all good library service, can build the desired image: The library is progressive and forward looking. It is a useful institution staffed by skilled people who are also newsworthy. It is a credit to the community. It continually expands to keep up with contemporary needs.

Librarians should establish good relations with news editors. They probably agree with the library's objectives and would like to help, but their job is to print news, not propaganda. Appointments to see them should be made and the library program discussed with them. Their deadlines should be learned and observed. Editors will of course expect copy in proper format—a typed, double-spaced original on the library letterhead with the telephone number and name of the public relations person and the release date. Standard newspaper style with accurate names, dates, addresses, spellings, and times should be used.

Radio news editors should receive news releases of activities which may fit into their programming scope. As with tele-

Part 4

Name of institution: STEVENSON PUBLIC LIBRARY   Date of writing:

Release date: FOR IMMEDIATE RELEASE   9/25/73

NEWS RELEASE

Questions about the progress of any bill before the Illinois
General Assembly can now be answered by the staff of the Stevenson
Public Library, according to Librarian James McKeever. In addition,
copies of bills can be examined in the library as soon as they are
available from the State Library.

This new service, provided by public libraries participating in
the State Library program, was funded by the General Assembly last year.
It will be in effect whenever the legislature is in session.

"We hope that this service will encourage our citizens to become
more involved in the legislative process," McKeever said. "We can
provide the basic ingredient--information."

-30-

For further information contact: James McKeever
                                  Stevenson Public Library
                                  221 Lincoln Avenue
                                  Lincoln, Illinois 60801
                                  (312) 555-1212

Fig. 2. Sample news release

vision, the proportion of their time available for local news is limited. Programming for the electronic media is demanding, and ideas for programs should be presented to the person who handles public service programming for the station.

Live copy to be read by an announcer (with a slide for television) should be discussed with news editors. They may be set up to use nothing but tapes or films which need to be prepared on a highly professional scale. This is another case in which it is advisable to seek professional help; a library can be much more successful by cooperating with others. Two groups, the American Association of School Librarians and the twenty-two public library systems in New York state, for example, have each developed radio and television spots to be used in a wide geographical area.

Publications and exhibits can be used to extend the usefulness of the library and interpret it both internally and externally. Pains should be taken to accomplish these with taste and skill. Here again is a case in which professional assistance is valuable. It may be sought among friends of the library or volunteers if the budget does not provide for this kind of skill.

In the development of the public relations program, as with other library activities, assistance from consultants at the state library level should be sought. They serve as a clearinghouse of ideas for effective policies and programs and can give much sound advice. Also, librarians sometimes forget to use their own collections and seek materials on all of these ideas in their shelves and files. If the supply is inadequate, a helpful comprehensive bibliography is *Public Relations: Information Sources* (vol. 22 of Management Information Guide series, [Detroit: Gale Research, 1970]).

Membership in local industrial editors groups or the local chapter of the Public Relations Society of America can provide an opportunity for exchange of ideas with others in the field.

All of the activities above are directed toward building a firm base of support that will stand by the library when a campaign for expansion is mounted, when salary schedules need upgrading, or when the library comes under attack for any reason. As for intellectual freedom, if the library has devoted ninety percent of its efforts to good performance and the remaining ten percent to effective interpretation, it should be able to meet the challenges which come its way with a well-understood materials selection policy based on sound principles, a planned response to complaints, and the support of many allies.

The Censor:
His Motives and Tactics

The term "censor" often evokes the mental picture of an irrational, belligerent individual. Such a picture, however, is misleading. In most cases, the one to bring a complaint to the library is a concerned parent or a citizen sincerely interested in the future well-being of the community. Although the complainant may not have a broad knowledge of literature or of the principles of freedom of expression, his motives in questioning a book or other library material are seldom unusual. Any number of reasons are given for recommending that certain material be removed from the library. The complainant may believe that the materials will corrupt children and adolescents, offend the sensitive or unwary reader, or undermine basic values and beliefs. Sometimes, because of these reasons, he may argue that the materials are of no interest or value to the community.

Although an attempt to stereotype the censor would be unfair, one generalization can be made: Regardless of specific motives, all would-be censors share one belief—that they can recognize "evil" and that other people must be protected from it. The censor does not necessarily believe his own morals should be protected, but he does feel compelled to save his fellows.

WHY CENSORSHIP?

In general, there are four basic motivational factors which may lie behind the censor's actions. The four motivations are by no means mutually exclusive; indeed, they often merge, both in outward appearance and in the censor's mind.

Family values. In some cases, the censor may feel threatened by changes in what to him is the accepted, traditional way of life. Changes in attitudes toward the family and related customs are naturally reflected in library materials, thus mistakenly leading people to believe that the materials themselves constitute a threat. Explicitly sexual works, in particular, are often viewed as obvious causes of repeated deviation from the norm. Because they challenge his values, the censor may want to protect his children from exposure to works dealing frankly with sexual topics and themes.

Political views. Changes in the political structure can be equally threatening. The censor may view a work that advocates radical change as subversive. (The fact that such works have been seen as attacking basic values is confirmed by the number of attempts to label library materials with such broad terms as "communistic," "un-American," or "un-godly.") If these works also contain less than polite language, it will not be difficult for the censor to formulate an attack on the grounds of obscenity in addition to—and sometimes to cover-up—objections on political grounds.

Religion. The censor may also view explicitly sexual works and politically unorthodox ideas as attacks on what he takes to be most basic: his religious faith. Antireligious works, or materials that the censor considers damaging to his own religious beliefs, cause concern about a society he sees becoming more and more hostile to religious training, and buttress his belief about society's steady disintegration.

Minority rights. Of course, not all censors are interested in preserving traditional values. Now the conservative censor has been joined by groups who want their own special group values recognized. For example, ethnic minorities and women struggling against long-established stereotypes are anxious to reject anything that represents a counter-value. And these groups, too, use the devices of the censor.

Whatever the censor's motives, his attempt to suppress certain library materials may also stem from a confused understanding of the role of the library and of the rights of other library users. The censor's concern about library materials shows that he views the library as an important social institution. But he may fail to see that the library fulfills its obligations to the community it serves by providing materials presenting all points of view, and that it is not the function of the library to screen materials according to arbitrary standards of acceptability. The censor may think that it is the role of the library to support certain values or causes, which are of course his values and his causes.

In the United States, under the First Amendment, no citizen and no librarian can properly assume that it is his duty or right to restrict or suppress legally protected expressions of ideas. The censor may not understand that his request that certain works be labeled or restricted would, if fulfilled, lead to an abridgement of the rights of other library users.

THE CENSOR IN ACTION

A censorship incident usually begins with a library user's complaint about specific library materials. In general, the immediate aim of the complainant is to inform the library that the materials in question are unacceptable. In some cases, the complainant may assume that the library will immediately agree that the materials are not appropriate and should not be in the library.

The censor may want to state publicly that he has found "objectionable" materials in the library and may attend a meeting of the library board to announce his "discovery." Those sections of the work that he considers especially offensive may be read aloud or distributed in writing to the library board, the local press, and the public. He may also go one step further and organize an ad hoc censorship organization. Even if an ad hoc group is loosely organized, the censors could use it effectively to promote a statement of purposes among other community groups, to conduct a letter-to-the-editor campaign, and to circulate petitions. The organization could also influence public funding, the appointment of the library director, and the appointment or election of library board members.

Although most censorship incidents begin with an objection to a specific work, if the censor is unsuccessful in getting the item banned he may turn his efforts to library policy. If he cannot bring about a change in the library's policy on materials selection and distribution, he may then ask that the library establish a closed shelf or adopt a policy of restricted access.

OPPOSING THE CENSOR

Well in advance of the appearance of the censor, a materials selection program, a procedure for handling complaints, and a public relations program will, of course, have been established. After the censor comes, censorship of library materials can be resisted by informing a number of key sources: (1) community leaders and community organizations who would support the position of the library; (2) local news media whose editorial support would be valuable; (3) other librarians in the community and state whose support could then be available if needed; (4) the publisher of the challenged work who may have on file all its reviews and may also be interested in the legal questions raised by such practices as labeling and restricted access; (5) all library staff members and the governing board; (6) the State Intellectual Freedom Committee; and (7) ALA's Office for Intellectual Freedom.

A censorship attempt presents the library with a good opportunity to explain the philosophy of intellectual freedom which underlies library service in the United States.

For example, the library should prepare an article for local newspapers explaining the role of the library and its commitment to the "Library Bill of Rights." The article can emphasize the importance of the freedom to read as established by the First Amendment. And the article can ask people whether they want any Big Brother to determine what materials will be available to them.

It is important to keep in mind that not every attempt to resist censorship will be successful; in many cases, developments will take a discouraging turn. However, it is certain that if the library is not prepared to offer any resistance, no battle will be won. And every battle won will contribute to establishing the library as an institution for free citizens in an open society.

Addendum: Participants in Ad Hoc Antipornography Organizations

Researchers for the Commission on Obscenity and Pornography tried to answer the question, What kinds of people become involved in ad hoc antipornography organizations? To do this the investigators questioned forty-nine persons who supported a community censorship organization, twenty-six persons from a contrasting, anticensorship group, and a control group. Some of the findings were as follows:

	Against Pornography	Against Censoring Pornography	Control Group
Demographic characteristics			
Average age	41.1	36.6	41.3
Attendance at church worship services:			
twice a week or more	48.9%	3.8%	18.4%
rarely or never	2.0	44.0	10.5
Highest level of education:			
completed high school	1.1%	0.0%	10.5%
completed college	14.3	0.0	21.1
graduate degree	14.3	73.1	21.1

The information presented here has been abstracted from Louis A. Zurcher and Robert G. Cushing, "Participants in Ad Hoc Antipornography Organizations," in *Technical Report of the Commission on Obscenity and Pornography*, vol. 5 (Washington: Govt. Printing Office, n.d.), p. 143–215.

Part 4

	Against Pornography	Against Censoring Pornography	Control Group
Political characteristics			
Interest in politics:			
very little	14.3%	0.0%	7.9%
some interest	26.5	19.2	42.1
high interest	59.2	76.9	44.7
Voting in local elections:			
rarely	2.0%	7.7%	2.6%
sometimes	0.0	0.0	10.5
frequently	98.0	92.3	68.4
Voting in national elections:			
rarely	2.0%	3.8%	2.6%
sometimes	0.0	0.0	0.0
frequently	98.0	96.2	78.9
Liberal or conservative preference:			
conservative	69.4%	0.0%	71.1%
liberal	22.4	88.5	18.4
moderate	6.1	11.5	2.6
Perceptions of pornography			
Effects of pornography:			
encourages violence	18.4%	0.0%	2.6%
encourages sexual deviance	6.1	7.7	7.9
degrades and abuses individual	24.5	3.8	21.1
has positive effects	0.0	19.2	2.6
"Sexual revolution" and pornography:			
there is no revolution	20.4%	26.9%	31.6%
there is a revolution and pornography is the cause	18.4	7.7	13.2
there is a revolution and pornography is the effect	16.3	15.4	10.5
there is a revolution, but pornography is not related	6.1	26.9	7.9

Generally speaking, the investigators found that persons active in antipornography censorship organizations tended to be middle-aged and family oriented. Most were engaged in nonprofessional white-collar work or small business jobs and tended to like their work. Despite the stereotype of "little old ladies in tennis shoes," they were just as likely to be male as female.

Members of opposing anticensorship organizations, on the other hand, were somewhat younger, had more formal schooling, and were less religiously and family oriented. Many were reared in large cities, and they tended to be politically liberal.

One unexpected finding of the investigation was that members of the censorship organizations did not experience feelings of powerlessness or alienation. Because of the comparative rigidity of their standards, however, they were inclined to be somewhat intolerant. Members of the anticensorship organizations, on the other hand, did feel powerless and alienated. (They were, however, in the minority in generally conservative communities.) On the whole, they were less authoritarian and dogmatic and more tolerant.

On the issue of pornography itself, members of the censorship organizations felt that "objectionable" materials presented a social problem. Their definition of pornography usually included specific references to nudity, depictions of "normal" and "abnormal" sexual activity, and the like. Most members of the opposing groups also felt that pornography was a social problem, but less serious or urgent than other problems. These people gave relativistic, "eye-of-the-beholder" definitions of pornography.

Intellectual Freedom and the Law

Librarians and Their Legislators

Eileen D. Cooke

Librarians are more qualified than many other citizens to work fruitfully with their legislators at local, state, and national levels. Legislators do respond to pressures. These may be the pressures of numbers—the almost irresistible force of massive public opinion opposing or supporting a measure. But legislators also respond—and to a greater degree than many realize—to the pressures of facts, logical reasoning, and intangible factors. Pressures like these are qualitative, yet no less effective. One good argument, one well-documented presentation, one staunch friend in a strategic position can accomplish more than great numbers on the other side of the question.

As a result, although librarians are not numerous, they can be and often are strikingly successful in their participation in the legislative process. They are accustomed to marshalling information, which is half the battle in a legislative contest. Their dedication to the public good is generally unquestioned, so that their support of or opposition to a measure is accepted by most legislators as soundly motivated, not for personal advantage. Moreover, librarians have many friends and allies, who are more numerous than themselves and hence count for more in the political scales. Librarians can work with groups representing educators and educational institutions, for example, or with groups representing children or parents or scholars—all groups that share or can be persuaded to share a legislative goal in common with librarians.

Eileen D. Cooke is Director of the American Library Association Washington Office.

SPECIFIC FACTS ABOUT THE
LEGISLATIVE SITUATION

The first step, once a legislative committee or subcommittee has been organized, is to inform leaders and membership alike of the specific facts regarding the legislative situation. With respect to the U.S. Congress, this is accomplished by close attention to the *ALA Washington Newsletter* and other communications from the ALA Washington Office appearing, for example, in *American Libraries*. The task is much more difficult at state or local levels, for what is needed is not the sort of general information reported in newspapers but much more detailed reports. The *Newsletter on Intellectual Freedom* is a principal source of news relating specifically to activities in this area. Accurate and timely information about a proposal is essential if an individual or organization is to take effective action:

> Who is sponsoring what measures? (More must be known about the sponsor than his name and home-town.)
>
> What committee is he on?
>
> What is his political situation?
>
> What are his views?
>
> To whom is he responsive?
>
> What is his background? (What libraries has he used?)

It may be, for example, that he will appreciate the implications of a pending measure much more readily if these are explained to him in terms of law libraries rather than in terms of public or school libraries. This is the sort of information that must be collected and collated and made easily available with respect to as many legislators as possible.

In regard to the measure itself, a thorough analysis must be made. If it involves First Amendment issues, the analysis must obviously be made by someone qualified to comment on this aspect. If it is a proposed appropriation, the analysis must indicate the probable effects of enactment—what services would be affected by a reduction of funds or what services could be expanded with an increase? The analysis will suggest potential allies to join the effort to enact or to defeat the measure. It will also suggest the best arguments in favor of or against the measure.

LEGISLATIVE STRATEGY AND TIMING

Next there is the question of legislative strategy and timing. Here one must rely on friends in the legislature. They will know the many other factors that are involved with the fate of the bill of concern:

> What is the workload of the committee to which it has been referred?
>
> When can the committee turn its attention to your measure?
>
> What is the sentiment of the chairman of the committee with respect to this bill?
>
> What is the sentiment of the committee as a whole?

Some of this information can be obtained through previously established contacts with the legislators, but other information is best obtained firsthand by the legislators themselves. Thousands of bills are introduced each year; however, relatively few are enacted into law.

Only a few legislators will take a strong interest in library legislation, some because they have a personal interest, perhaps because of a concerned relative or friend, and others because they are on the committee handling bills of this type. These members will not only advise the library of the prospects of its bill, but will also offer counsel regarding the strategy to be adopted, the position to be taken in hearings, the nature of the testimony to be presented, the kind of witnesses to be secured, and the like. This advice is invaluable and should be heeded.

CONTACT BETWEEN LIBRARIANS AND LEGISLATORS

It is implicit in all that has been said thus far that considerable contact between librarians and legislators is a must during this process. All persons who are active in legislative affairs will be seeing legislators frequently and, in time, they

5

will know many of them well as individuals. Ideally, one should see his legislators when they are "at home," that is, in their district rather than at the state capital or in Washington. One should be familiar with their home office and should be acquainted with their home office staff. All congressmen maintain at least one office in their district, and the staffs of these offices can reveal when their boss will be at that office and available to citizens who want to meet with him.

To meet with a legislator, a librarian should make an appointment, then leave little to chance. He should plan what to say, be well-versed on the bill being discussed, and, if possible, prepare a brief memorandum, preferably only one page, covering the relevant points. (A copy should be left with the legislator.) A fact sheet on the library, listing its strengths, its problems, and its prospects would also be valuable. During the meeting, he should give the legislator ample opportunity for questioning, ask him which member of his staff to keep in touch with when he is unavailable, and request to be put on his mailing list to keep abreast of his activities. Similarly, it is important that the library keep the legislator informed of the library's activities, invite him to functions or special activities when this is appropriate, or ask him to join a board or advisory group if this is feasible.

Meetings with legislators need not be frequent. Usually one meeting before a legislative session begins, preferably when he is at home, and perhaps one more meeting during the legislative session when an important measure is at a decisive point, will be sufficient. Of course, at each session of the legislature there are new members, and these should be visited to ascertain their viewpoint, their interests, and their potential position vis-à-vis the legislation that concerns you.

Personal contacts with legislators should precede letters and other less personal communications whenever possible. Letters will prove much more effective if they are read by a legislator who has met the sender. Ideally, each legislator should have a flow of contacts with one or more librarians from his district or state, a few letters each year, and at least one visit, either on his turf or the library's during each legislative session.

Representative Morris K. Udall of Arizona devoted the January 20, 1967, issue of his newsletter to "Some Suggestions on Writing Your Congressman." His comments are equally applicable to members of state or local legislatures.

6

"On several occasions I can testify that a single, thoughtful, factually persuasive letter did change my mind or cause me to initiate a review of a previous judgment," he wrote. "Nearly every day my faith is renewed by one or more informative and helpful letters giving me a better understanding of the thinking of my constituents."

The gist of Representative Udall's advice to those writing to him and to other legislators is that letters should be timely, constructive, reasoned and short. He and other legislators like to get letters thanking them for the positions they have taken. They don't like letters threatening or berating them, nor those that demand a commitment to a position before all sides have been heard or before the pending bill has been modified, as most are in advance of a decisive or final vote.

BIPARTISANSHIP

Neither party should be neglected, of course. Today's minority in the legislature may be tomorrow's majority. It is rare, indeed, that all one's foes or friends will be found in one party. Therefore, librarians will want to cultivate legislators of both parties. Surprisingly, few librarians have met their congressmen, senators, or state legislators. Even fewer have developed a continuing correspondence or series of visits with their legislators. Yet, these are the people who will have much to say and do about the future of nearly every library.

NETWORK APPROACH

A network approach is required to bring maximum constituent effort to bear upon the Congress, the state legislatures, the national and state administrations, and appropriate regulatory agencies in support of library services. Proponents of library-related legislation must develop clear lines of communication and action, and avoid duplication of effort. This means strengthening ALA's working relationships with other national associations and with state chapters; strengthening state chapters' relationships with each other; and integrating activities aimed at federal, state and local legislation. For

7

Part 5

How to Write A Letter to Your Congressman

The most frequently used, correct forms of address are:

To your senator:	To your representative:
The Honorable (full name)	The Honorable (full name)
United States Senate	U.S. House of Representatives
Washington, D.C. 20510	Washington, D.C. 20515

Dear Senator _____ : Dear Mr. _____ :

"Sincerely yours" is in good taste as a complimentary close. Remember to sign your given name and surname. If you use a title in your signature (Miss, Mrs., etc.), be sure to enclose it in parentheses.

Forms similar to the above, addressed to your state capital, are appropriate for your state representatives and senators.

Where possible use your official letterhead. If this is not in order, and you write as an individual, use plain white bond paper, and give your official title following your signature as a means of identification and to indicate your competency to speak on the subject.

REMEMBER

1. your Congressman likes to hear opinions from home and wants to be kept informed of conditions in the district. Base your letter on your own pertinent experiences and observations.

2. if writing about a specific bill, describe it by number or its popular name. Your Congressman has thousands of bills before him in the course of a year, and cannot always take time to figure out to which one you are referring.

3. he likes intelligent, well-thought-out letters which present a definite position, even if he does not agree with it.

4. even more important and valuable to him is a concrete statement of the reasons for your position—particularly if you are writing about a

Fig. 3. Suggestions for writing letters

8

field in which you have specialized knowledge. He has to vote on many matters with which he has had little or no first-hand experience. Some of the most valuable help he gets in making up his own mind comes from facts presented in letters from persons who have knowledge in the field.

5. short letters are almost always best. Members of Congress receive many, many letters each day, and a long one may not get as prompt a reading as a brief statement.

6. letters should be timed to arrive while the issue is alive. If your Congressman is a member of the committee considering the bill, he will appreciate having your views while the bill is before him for study and action.

7. your Congressman likes to know when he has done something of which you approve. He is quite as human as you, so don't forget to follow through with a thank-you letter.

AVOID

1. letters that merely demand or insist that he vote for or against a certain bill; or that tell him how you want him to vote, but not why. He has no way of knowing whether your reasons are good or bad, and therefore he is not greatly influenced.

2. threats of defeat at the next election.

3. boasts of how influential the writer is in his own community.

4. asking him to commit himself on a particular bill before the committee in charge of the subject has had a chance to hear the evidence and make its report.

5. form letters or letters which include excerpts from other letters on the same subject.

6. writing to a Congressman from another district, except when the letter deals with a matter which is before a committee of which he is a member. Otherwise, Congressional courtesy makes him refer letters from non-constituents to the proper persons.

7. writing too many letters on the same subject. Quality, not quantity, is what counts.

example, a state legislative "watchdog"—the person (or persons) who keeps track of all legislation introduced—is imperative, particularly in regard to intellectual freedom. Many bills affecting this area of concern are nonlibrary measures, and too often librarians learn of them only after the fact. Someone else in each state should be responsible for keeping track of face-to-face contacts with legislators. Contacts should be reported, albeit informally, with some indication of the legislator's response to the position or concern conveyed in talking with him. These reports will indicate which members must still be visited as well as which ones require other, perhaps more persuasive, visits by librarians. One legislator may respond to a visit from a representative of his alma mater, another, to a visit by a large group or to a request to address a meeting of librarians and their friends. Knowledge about the proposed measure, followed by individual attention and treatment of legislators, is the way to success.

COALITION

As the librarian becomes more active in the processes discussed above, he will find that other groups share his objectives or can be persuaded to do so. These actual or potential allies should be sought and worked with. They may be education organizations, other professional societies, trade associations, or civic groups. Chapters of the American Civil Liberties Union and state and local intellectual freedom units of other national organizations are obvious allies. They may work with the library on all the measures of concern, or their interest in its legislative objectives may be limited to one bill alone. In any event, the library should make contact and keep in touch with the leadership and the legislative activists of these organizations.

It should be recognized that American politics is coalition politics, for the most part, rather than confrontation politics. Candidates strive to satisfy as many elements of their constituency as possible. Each party seeks the support of as many segments of the electorate as possible. It is therefore very helpful to demonstrate to legislators that many other organizations are joining or supporting the library's efforts. If the library takes a position on a bill, it is helpful if the statement of position is signed by many other organizations.

Obviously, these relationships, too, must be seeded and nurtured.

Public opinion should not be overlooked. In addition to letters to legislators, there should be timely, concise, and cogent letters to newspapers and other publications. This is another instance in which the library's public relations program can bear fruit. If an editorial or columnist calls for lower government expenditures, a letter should point out the effects of a cutback on the library's users. If a pending legislative measure is endorsed, or opposed, a letter should present the librarian's position on the issue. Letters should be directed, in particular, to the publications of greatest influence in the area. With a strong working relationship developed with the press, the chances of having the library's materials published are much stronger. If they are published, a wide audience will be reached. Even if they are unpublished, it is sure that they were read and perhaps remembered in the editorial offices.

PERSISTENCE, PERSUASIONS, AND PLANNING

Each step in the process of achieving rapport with legislators is simple in itself; the power of these efforts is in their cumulative impact and their multiplication when performed by many others. In this process, each participant is significant. The story of the lobbying once endured by former Senator Mike Monroney of Oklahoma is instructive with respect to this point. Years ago the Senator sponsored a bill that was favored by the oil industry. Mrs. Monroney, however, was personally opposed to the bill, believing it to be detrimental to the consumer. For weeks she tried to persuade her husband to withdraw his support for the bill. He remained unpersuaded, however, and in the end the bill was enacted by Congress.

Nevertheless, Mrs. Monroney had the last word. Convinced that she was right and her husband wrong, she contacted her friend, Bess Truman, and asked the First Lady to lobby her husband. Persuaded, Mrs. Truman agreed to speak to the President about the bill. She did, and that is said to have been a major reason for President Truman's veto of Senator Monroney's bill.

Part 5

In the legislative process, as in so many other matters, where there is a will, there is always a way. Persuasion plays an important role in the political process, but planning and persistence are equally essential for substantial success. Politics is called the art of the possible, and that is the art of compromise. Progress often comes one step at a time.

Assistance from ALA

What ALA Can Do to Help the Library Combat Censorship

The American Library Association maintains a broadly based program for the promotion and defense of intellectual freedom. The program is composed of the Intellectual Freedom Committee; the Office for Intellectual Freedom; the Program of Action for Mediation, Arbitration, and Inquiry; and the Freedom to Read Foundation.

ESTABLISHMENT OF POLICY

According to its revised statement of responsibility, approved by the Council in 1970, the purpose of the Intellectual Freedom Committee is "to recommend such steps as may be necessary to safeguard the rights of library users, libraries, and librarians, in accordance with the First Amendment to the United States Constitution and the Library Bill of Rights as adopted by the ALA Council; to work closely with the Office for Intellectual Freedom and with other units and officers of the Association in matters touching intellectual freedom and censorship."[1]

The first part of this responsibility is discharged in large measure through the recommendation of policies concerning intellectual freedom to the ALA Council. Council approved policy statements on such matters as free access to libraries for minors, labeling of library materials, censorship of library materials because of alleged racism or sexism, and the like, not only provide the librarian with concrete guidelines for establishing policy within his own library, but also establish a professional code to whose defense the Association is committed. It is on the basis of such policy statements that the

1. *American Libraries* 3, no.10:1048 (Nov. 1972).

Association can come to the aid of a librarian whose professional conduct in defense of the principles of intellectual freedom is challenged.

EDUCATIONAL AND PROFESSIONAL SUPPORT

The basic program of the Intellectual Freedom Committee is educational in nature. The most effective safeguards for the rights of library users and librarians are an informed public and a library profession aware of repressive activities and how to combat them. Toward this end, the administrative arm of the Intellectual Freedom Committee, the Office for Intellectual Freedom, attempts to implement ALA policies on intellectual freedom and to educate librarians to the importance of the concept. The Office maintains a wide-ranging program of educational and informational publications, projects, and services. In addition to publication of the bimonthly *Newsletter on Intellectual Freedom* and the monthly *OIF Memorandum*, the Office distributes documents, articles, and ALA policies concerning intellectual freedom. As special circumstances require, materials regularly distributed by the Office are augmented. During nationwide controversies concerning individual titles, press clippings, editorials, and public statements detailing the ways various libraries around the country handled requests to remove specific materials are compiled and sent out to others with problems. Such special packets are publicized through *American Libraries*, the *OIF Memorandum*, the *Newsletter on Intellectual Freedom*, the library and educational press, and special mailings.

The Office for Intellectual Freedom also provides advice and consultation to librarians in the throes of potential or actual censorship problems. Every effort is made to provide information or give other assistance. Sometimes this assistance takes the form of a formal ALA position statement defending the principles of intellectual freedom, and sometimes the Office ghosts such a statement for the use of the librarian involved in the controversy. Other times, such assistance requires names of persons available to offer testimony before library boards. In extreme cases, it demands visiting the community to review the problem first-hand and to provide moral and professional support for the librarian and the board. The alternative(s) chosen is always the prerogative of the individual requesting assistance. If a censorship problem arises, librarians should contact the Office for Intellectual Freedom (50 East Huron Street, Chicago, Illinois 60611; phone 312-944-6780).

COMBATTING REPRESSIVE LEGISLATION

Repressive legislation on such matters as obscenity and material deemed harmful to minors can severely restrict the activities of the librarian who strives to provide service in accordance with the principles of the "Library Bill of Rights." Therefore, the ALA, through the Intellectual Freedom Committee and the Office for Intellectual Freedom, as well as the Freedom to Read Foundation, often supply testimony, either singly or jointly, supporting or opposing proposed legislation affecting the principles of intellectual freedom as applied to library service. Pending legislation in the United States Congress is frequently brought to the attention of these groups by the ALA Washington Office. With the assistance of ALA legal counsel, the Office for Intellectual Freedom will analyze any proposed state or local statute affecting intellectual freedom which is brought to its attention.

In furtherance of its purpose "to support the right of libraries to include in their collections and to make available to the public any creative work which they may legally acquire," the Freedom to Read Foundation combats through the courts statutes in force that limit or make illegal application of the principles of intellectual freedom. Librarians affected by repressive statutes in force should contact the Freedom to Read Foundation.

FINANCIAL AND LEGAL ASSISTANCE

According to its constitution, one purpose of the Freedom to Read Foundation is "to supply legal counsel, which counsel may or may not be directly employed by the Foundation, and otherwise to provide support to such libraries and librarians as are suffering legal injustices by reason of their defense of freedom of speech and freedom of the press as guaranteed by law against efforts to subvert such freedoms through suppression or censorship. . . ." Librarians whose

5

professional positions and personal well-being are endangered because of their defense of intellectual freedom, and library boards, librarians, and library employees threatened with legal action on such grounds, should contact the Foundation.

Librarians requiring immediate financial aid should contact the LeRoy C. Merritt Humanitarian Fund. The Merritt Fund was established by the Freedom to Read Foundation's Board of Trustees in recognition of the need for support at the moment an individual finds his position in jeopardy or is fired in the cause of intellectual freedom. This special fund allows for immediate assistance even prior to the establishment of all pertinent facts in a particular case. Depending on the situation, grants can be made prior to establishment of claims that intellectual freedom is involved.

MEDIATION AND ARBITRATION

In June 1971, the ALA Council approved the "Program of Action for Mediation, Arbitration, and Inquiry," thus establishing a means for ALA to gather facts regarding violations of ALA policies concerning status, tenure, due process, fair employment practices, ethical considerations, and, certainly, the principles of intellectual freedom. When it receives a complaint, the Staff Committee on Mediation, Arbitration, and Inquiry attempts various means by which to effect a just resolution to the problem. If these efforts fail, a fact-finding team may be appointed and its reports reviewed by the staff committee. The staff committee may then recommend to the ALA Executive Board, which determines the final disposition of cases, one of the following actions:

1. Publication of a report that includes a statement of censure, indicating the strong disapproval of ALA because of a violation of one or more of the policies to which [the] Program of Action relates.

2. Suspension or expulsion from membership in ALA.

3. Listing of parties under censure in *American Libraries* as a warning to persons considering employment in a institution under censure that its practices and policies are in conflict with ALA policies concerning tenure, status, fair employment practices, due process, ethical practices, and/or the principles of intellectual freedom.

On the same page with such listings of censured libraries shall appear the following statement:

The fact that the name of an institution appears on the censured list of administrations does not establish a boycott of a library, nor does it visit censure on the staff. There is no obligation for ALA members to refrain from accepting appointment in censured libraries. The ALA advises only that librarians, before accepting appointments, seek information on present conditions from the Staff Committee on Mediation, Arbitration, and Inquiry at Headquarters.[2]

The ALA Executive Board determines the final disposition of cases handled by the Staff Committee.

Without these programs of support, the Association's call to all librarians to commit themselves to the principles of intellectual freedom would indeed be hypocrisy. Thus the Association makes every effort to maintain them and includes them among its highest priorities.

2. From "Program of Action for Mediation, Arbitration and Inquiry," adopted June 25, 1971, by the ALA Council.

Selected Readings

Anastaplo, George. *Constitutionalist: Notes on the First Amendment.* Dallas: Southern Methodist Univ. Pr., 1971.

Berns, Walter. *Freedom, Virtue, and the First Amendment.* Baton Rouge: Louisiana State Univ. Pr., 1957.

Blanshard, Paul. *The Right to Read: The Battle against Censorship.* Boston: Beacon Pr., 1955.

Boyer, Paul S. *Purity in Print: Book Censorship in America.* New York: Scribner, 1968.

Broun, Heywood, and Leech, Margaret. *Anthony Comstock: Roundsman of the Lord.* New York: Literary Guild of America, 1927.

Busha, Charles H. *Freedom Versus Suppression and Censorship: With a Study of the Attitude of Midwestern Librarians and a Bibliography of Censorship.* Littleton, Colo.: Libraries Unlimited, 1972.

Combatting Undemocratic Pressures on Schools and Libraries: A Guide for Local Communities. New York: American Civil Liberties Union, 1964.

Craig, Alec. *Suppressed Books: A History of the Conception of Literary Obscenity.* Cleveland: World Publishing Co., 1963.

Downs, Robert B., ed. *The First Freedom.* Chicago: American Library Assn., 1960.

Ernst, Morris L., and Lindey, Alexander. *The Censor Marches On: Recent Milestones in the Administration of the Obscenity Law in the United States.* New York: Doubleday, 1940.

Ernst, Morris L., and Schwartz, Alan U. *Censorship: The Search for the Obscene.* New York: Macmillan, 1964.

Ernst, Morris L., and Seagle, William. *To the Pure . . . : A Study of Obscenity and the Censor.* New York: Viking, 1928.

Fellman, David. *The Censorship of Books.* Madison: Univ. of Wisconsin Pr., 1957.

Fiske, Marjorie. *Book Selection and Censorship: A Study of School and Public Libraries in California.* Berkeley: Univ. of California Pr., 1959.

Frank, John P., and Hogan, Robert F. *Obscenity, the Law, and the English Teacher.* Champaign, Ill.: National Council of Teachers of English, 1966.

Gardiner, Harold C., S. J. *Catholic Viewpoint on Censorship.* Garden City, N.Y.: Doubleday, Image Paperbacks, 1961.

Gellhorn, Walter. *Individual Freedom and Governmental Restraints.* Baton Rouge: Louisiana State Univ. Pr., 1956.

Haight, Anne Lyon. *Banned Books: Informal Notes on Some Books Banned for Various Reasons at Various Times and in Various Places.* 3d ed. New York: Bowker, 1970.

Haney, Robert W. *Comstockery in America.* Boston: Beacon Pr., 1960.

Hartogs, Renatus. *Four-Letter Word Games: The Psychology of Obscenity.* New York: Dell, 1968.

Hove, John, ed. *Meeting Censorship in the School: A Series of Case Studies.* Champaign, Ill.: National Council of Teachers of English, 1967.

Hutchison, E. R. *"Tropic of Cancer" on Trial: A Case History of Censorship.* New York: Grove Pr., 1968.

Hyde, H. Montgomery. *A History of Pornography.* New York: Farrar, 1964.

Intellectual Freedom Committee, American Library Association. *Freedom of Inquiry: Supporting the Library Bill of Rights.* Proceedings of the Conference on Intellectual Freedom, January 1965, Washington, D.C. Chicago: ALA, 1965.

Jackson, Holbrook. *The Fear of Books.* New York: Scribner, 1932.

Jennison, Peter. *Freedom to Read.* New York: Public Affairs Pamphlets, 1963.

Jones, Howard Mumford, ed. *Primer of Intellectual Freedom.* Cambridge: Harvard Univ. Pr., 1949.

Kerr, Walter. *Criticism and Censorship.* Milwaukee: Bruce Publishing Co., 1956.

Kirk, Russell. *Academic Freedom: An Essay in Definition.* Chicago: Henry Regnery Co., 1955.

Kronhausen, Eberhard, and Kronhausen, Phyllis. *Pornography and the Law: The Psychology of Erotic Realism and Pornography.* New York: Ballantine, 1959.

Kuh, Richard H. *Foolish Figleaves? Pornography in and out of Court.* New York: Macmillan, 1967.

Kujoth, Jean Spealman, ed. *Libraries, Readers, and Book Selection.* Metuchen, N. J.: Scarecrow Pr., 1969.

McCormick, John, and MacInnes, Mairi, eds. *Versions of Censorship: An Anthology.* Garden City, N.Y.: Doubleday, Anchor Paperbacks, 1962.

McKeon, Richard; Merton, Robert K.; and Gellhorn, Walter. *The Freedom to Read: Perspective and Program.* New York: Bowker, 1957.

Merritt, LeRoy Charles. *Book Selection and Intellectual Freedom.* New York: Wilson, 1970.

Moon, Eric, ed. *Book Selection and Censorship in the Sixties.* New York: Bowker, 1969.

Moore, Everett, ed. *Issues of Freedom in American Libraries.* Chicago: American Library Assn., 1964.

Murphy, Terrence J. *Censorship: Government and Obscenity.* Baltimore: Helicon, 1963.

Rembar, Charles. *The End of Obscenity.* New York: Random, 1968.

Report of the Commission on Obscenity and Pornography. New York: Random, 1970.

Rolph, C. H., ed. *Does Pornography Matter?* London: Routlege, 1961.

Rubin, David. *The Rights of Teachers.* American Civil Liberties Union Handbook. New York: Avon, 1972.

Street, Harry. *Freedom, the Individual, and the Law.* Baltimore: Penguin Books, 1963.

DATE DUE

GAYLORD			PRINTED IN U.S.A.